BY
JOHN C. BOWLING

WHAT A NOVICE CLIMBER LEARNED ABOUT LIFE ON MOUNT KILIMANJARO

BEACON HILL PRESS
OF KANSAS CITY

ISBN-13: 978-0-8341-2326-7
ISBN-10: 0-8341-2326-6

Cover Design: Brandon R. Hill
Interior Design: Sharon Page
Photo Credit p. 11: photos.com © 2007 JupiterImages Corporation

Library of Congress Cataloging-in-Publication Data

Bowling, John C., 1949-
    Making the climb : what a nonclimber learned about life on Mount Kilimanjaro / John C. Bowling.
        p. cm.
    Includes bibliographical references.
    ISBN-13: 978-0-8341-2326-7 (pbk.)
    ISBN-10: 0-8341-2326-6 (pbk.)
    1. Bowling, John C., 1949- 2. Spiritual biography. 3. Mountains—Religious aspects—Christianity.
4. Kilimanjaro, Mount (Tanzania) I. Title.

    BR1725.B65A3 2007
    276.78'26—dc22

                                                            2007017478

To

Leo, Vince, Scott,
Christian, Tim and Carey

Companions on the journey

All proceeds from the sale of this book are
donated to the general scholarship fund of
OLIVET NAZARENE UNIVERSITY
Bourbonnais, IL 60914
www.olivet.edu

CONTENTS

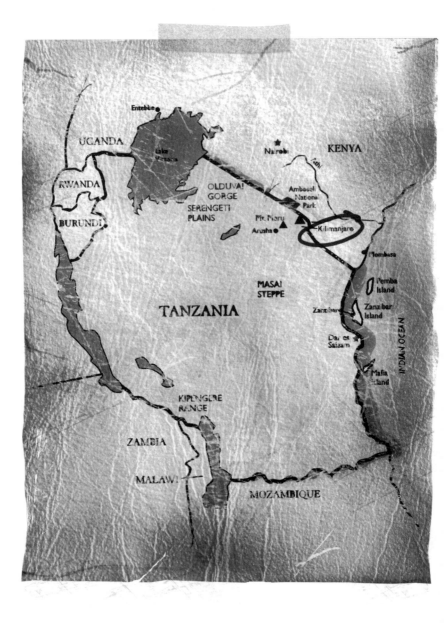

A PSALM FOR THE CLIMB

I lift up my eyes to the hills—
where does my help come from?
My help comes from the LORD,
the Maker of heaven and earth.

He will not let your foot slip—
he who watches over you will not slumber;
indeed, he who watches over Israel
will neither slumber nor sleep.

The LORD watches over you—
the LORD is your shade at your right hand;
the sun will not harm you by day,
nor the moon by night.

The LORD will keep you from all harm—
he will watch over your life;
the LORD will watch over your coming and going
both now and forevermore.
—Ps. 121

INTRODUCTION
LIFE IS FILLED WITH MOUNTAINS

The real voyage of discovery consists not in seeking new landscapes, but in having new eyes.
—Marcel Proust

It was just after dawn on a warm January day in 1986 when I first saw Kilimanjaro rising through the early morning mist, its gleaming white summit shining in the equatorial sun. I was on my first trip to East Africa. My companions and I had been in Nairobi, the capital city of Kenya, for about two weeks when, on a Saturday morning several hours before sunrise, we crowded into a well-traveled safari van to make the drive to the Amboseli game park on the Kenya-Tanzania border.

The small but beautiful Amboseli National Park is about 150 miles (240 km.) south from Nairobi. This wildlife paradise contains Kenya's largest herds of elephant, as well as giraffe, hippos, water buffalo, and the plains animals such as zebra, gazelle, and impala. There is also a large array of birdlife in and around the water areas. Yet the most striking feature of the Amboseli landscape, with its parched alkaline pan, strange mirages, and array of animals, is the glistening, majestic snowcap of Mount Kilimanjaro. It is the dominating backdrop to all one sees and senses.

On the drive from Nairobi, we crossed the Athi plains, home of the proud and colorful Maasai tribe. The Maasai is one of more than 50 tribes of native people who reside across East Africa. They have always been regarded as a special people. Their bright red robes and stately being set them apart visually. Spear in hand, they appear calm and courageous regardless of circumstances. Until recently, the only way for a Maasai boy to achieve warrior status was to single-handedly kill a lion with his spear.

While our van hummed along the narrow paved road a few hours south of the capital, the sky took on a faint golden glow as the sun began to peek one eye over the eastern horizon. Little by little through the early morning shadows we could see the Maasai already out walking with their cattle. Here and there we spotted their villages tucked into the thickets of the broad awakening landscape.

The Maasai do not have communities with permanent buildings. Instead, they construct an *enkang* (corral) for a group of interrelated families. The enkang is a circle of huts, one per family, enclosed by a circular fence of thornbushes. Women of each household construct the huts from cattle dung and clay.

These pastoral and somewhat nomadic people of the open plains subsist on their herds of cattle and goats. In common with the wildlife with which they coexist, the Maasai need a lot of land. Periodically, therefore, a family group will abandon its village and construct a new dwelling place in an area with better water and grazing.

Karen Blixen (Isak Dinesen), one of the first Europeans to write extensively about East Africa, made the following observation in her book *Out of Africa:*

> A Maasai warrior is a fine sight. Those young men have, to the utmost extent, that particular form of intelligence which we call chic; daring and wildly fantastical as they seem, they are still unswervingly true to their own nature, and to an immanent ideal. Their style is not an assumed manner, nor an imitation of a foreign perfection; it has grown from the inside, and is an expression of the race and

its history, and their weapons and finery are as much a part of their being as are a stag's antlers.[1]

Once it was fairly light, we pulled off the road and piled out of the van to stretch. The rays of the sun were already comfortably warm, yet the breeze was still cool from the night. The air was filled with the rich and pungent fragrance of the open savanna.

As my eyes began to adjust to the landscape, I saw in the distance a sight that nearly took my breath away. It was Mount Kilimanjaro. I stood and stared. The mountain had a regal presence. Not only did it seem to touch the sky, but it was broad and majestic with a bright tiara of white diamonds. It was still miles and miles away, yet I was drawn to it by the magnetism of its grandeur.

Created by fire and now crowned with ice, Mount Kilimanjaro rises 19,340 feet, making it the tallest peak in all of Africa and the highest freestanding volcano on earth. It rests on the vast East African plain as a solitary giant, standing guard, watching, casting its spell for hundreds of miles in all direc-

tions. It is a mountain of wonder and mystery unlike any other in the world.

That first glimpse of the mountain was 20 years ago. I have seen it since on return trips to Africa—but now I am going back, not to look at Kilimanjaro from a distance but to climb it; to stand, if I can, on the roof of Africa. Traveling with a professional guide, a small group of porters, and a handful of other climbers, I will attempt to reach Uhuru Peak, the summit of Kilimanjaro, by foot.

To scale Mount Kilimanjaro is like walking from the equator to the North Pole, that is, from the tropics to the tundra, in just one week. This arduous ascent will consist of nine days of climbing, camping, and mountaineering in the open air. The climb covers 65 miles through five climate zones. The journey begins in a lush tropical forest and makes its way, mile after mile, up out of the tangle of trees onto the high plains. It then passes the upper tree line to a heather zone and meanders up to an elevated alpine region.

Then comes the most difficult part of the climb—the lunarlike expanse of the upper mountain with its jagged, gleaming glaciers and temperatures well below freezing. The air is thin and the wind is harsh. If/when a climber makes it to this treacherous section, he or she will face the last two obstacles—to scale the rim of the volcanic crater and then to climb the remaining distance to the summit.

This will be an adventure of body, mind, and spirit for me unlike anything I have ever done—but there is more. I also view the mountain and the climb itself as metaphors for life as a whole. All people, young and old, have mountains to climb. Nearly every day we face issues, obstacles, opportunities, and challenges that dominate the landscape of simply being alive.

Life is filled with mountains.

The question lying at the heart of my climb is this: *What can be learned from climbing this mountain that might help me reach other goals and conquer other mountains?* I expect the value of the Kilimanjaro climb to lie well beyond the days spent on the mountain. Those hours, while rich and full, will be relatively brief; the lessons learned from the mountain may last a lifetime.

Each of us sees the world through a prism created by our personal set of experiences, perceptions, and culture. Most people have some desire to press beyond the confines of daily life and discover more about the world around them and the world within. To experience life differently, even for a few weeks, can enrich one's understanding of life from that moment forward.

The trip will also be a spiritual journey, a retreat to the mountain for meditation, prayer, and spiritual growth. Time for serious spiritual reflection is increasingly difficult to find in the midst of 21st-century life. It is my desire that by pulling away from a crowded schedule and a demanding lifestyle, I will be able to sense the presence of God in new ways.

I invite you to make this journey with me. Clear your schedule; pull on your boots and grab your backpack as we set off to climb one of the world's most magnificent peaks. Don't look down!

SECTION ONE

THE PRINCIPLE OF PREPARATION

The ancient philosophers got it right. Plato said, "The beginning is the most important part of the work."

And it was Aristotle who noted, "Well begun is half done."

To climb any mountain calls for preparation.

1
THE MOUNTAIN

A vast mountain of gold and silver in the far interior,
the approach to which was guarded by evil spirits.
—Johann Rebmann, May 11, 1848

Mount Kilimanjaro stands on an otherwise featureless part of
the East African plateau, in northern Tanzania just south of the
Kenya border, side by side with the smaller Mount Meru. Both
mountains are extinct volcanoes, with Kilimanjaro actually being
the agglomeration of three distinct volcanoes. These peaks
were formed geologically as part of a wide, violent movement
that also created the Great Rift Valley that stretches north and
south for hundreds of miles across East Africa.

Kilimanjaro conforms to our childlike notions of what a
mountain should look like. It is high, wide, and handsome—a
vast triangle rising up from the flat earth. Its sides accelerate exponentially
as they press skyward toward the towering, broad
summit. The anthropologist Charles Dundas, writing in 1924,
noted that he had seen Kilimanjaro from a distance of 120 miles.

It was in 1848 that Christian missionaries reported seeing a
huge, snowcapped mountain, which they said was called the
Mountain of the Caravans by Arab traders from Zanzibar who
used the peak as a landmark while crossing the interior. Initially
Europeans refused to believe that snow could exist at the equator.
It was not until the Royal Geographical Society sent an expedition
in 1861 to confirm its existence that the majestic Mount
Kilimanjaro became widely known outside of East Africa.

ORIGIN OF THE NAME KILIMANJARO

There are many explanations for how the mountain got its name, yet little common agreement. Mountain of Greatness, Mountain of Whiteness, and Mountain of the Caravans are all names that have been used to describe the mountain. These have been derived from the Swahili, Chagga, and Machame dialects.

Most linguistic researchers think the name has some direct relationship to the Swahili word *kilima*, which means "top of the hill." The second portion, *njaro*, presumably refers in some way to the snow. There is also a claim that the word *kilemakyaro* exists in the Chagga language, meaning "impossible journey"; although this is thought to have come about as a consequence rather than a precedent.

HISTORY

The myth of such a mountain was a great source of ancient fascination. In the second century A.D., Ptolemy, the Greek astronomer and cartographer, wrote of mysterious lands to the south of modern-day Somalia that contained a "great snow mountain." He may have gained this information from the Phoenicians, who had circumnavigated Africa by this date. He may also have been drawing on ancient Egyptian writings telling of the great expeditions of the pharaoh Hatshepsut, whose ships had traded on the Swahili Coast. Either way, Ptolemy's account stands as the first documented report of Africa's highest mountain, Kilimanjaro.

The next thousand years or so brought no mention of this great mountain. However, the coast of East Africa rose in prominence as a trading route following the establishment of Arab rule in the 6th century. The main hub of activity centered on the island of Zanzibar and the immediate mainland known at the time as Zinj. The Arabs had at their disposal an almost unlimited supply of ivory, gold, rhinoceros horn, and a far more lucrative and mobile commodity—slaves.

While surely the great slave caravans that ventured far into the interior would have passed close by the mountain to collect water from the permanent streams, it was the Chinese traders of the 12th century that were next to record observations of a great mountain to the west of Zanzibar. That reference was never widely circulated, and so Kilimanjaro was to remain a mountain of myth and superstition throughout the centuries—one of the great secrets of the dark continent.

It was Christian missionary zeal and, later, the desire to find the source of the Nile during the mid-19th century that drove European explorers and geographers to head inland toward the mysterious mountain.

Johann Ludwig Krapf and Johann Rebmann

In January 1844, with the backing of the London-based Church Missionary Society (CMS), Johann Ludwig Krapf, a minister, and his wife, Rosine, arrived in Zanzibar. Krapf had a dream to link the west and east coasts of Africa with a chain of Christian missionary outposts. But it was not until he arrived in Africa that he discovered that his high ambitions, conceived in the comfort of Europe, were not going to be so easily realized in the field.

In March of that year, Ludwig and Rosine moved to Mombasa on the eastern coast of Kenya, where Krapf was to suffer a major test of his faith. Rosine was pregnant when they left Zanzibar. She gave birth to a daughter on July 6. Both she and her husband were suffering from malaria. The baby was born well, but Rosine's health quickly worsened. On July 9, she became convinced that she was going to die and said, "I am not worthy of being in the midst of paradise, but only let me have a little place on its skirts."

Kraft consoled her as much as possible. He lay on a couch beside her bed, himself so weakened with fever that when Rosine died it was not until some hours later that he could raise himself to care for the baby. His daughter died of fever five days later and was buried beside her mother. He wrote back to the CMS committee chairman saying, "Tell them, my dear Sir, that there is on the East African coast a lonely grave."

Krapf was plunged into depression and suffered alone for two years. Yet during those dark days he translated the New Testament into Swahili, compiled a short grammar and dictionary, and made a few exploratory journeys. But there were no converts to Christianity.

After those two years of lonely suffering, help arrived in the person of Swiss missionary Johann Rebmann, whose fresh enthusiasm was able finally to rekindle Krapf's ambition to link the two coasts. Together they became convinced that God would give them a harvest for their labor.

Soon Rebmann also contracted malaria, yet together the two missionaries set off for Rabbai Mpia, a Wanika village some distance from Mombasa. Very weak and scarcely able to travel, they pressed on. "Never was a mission begun in such weakness," wrote Krapf, "but so it was to be, that we might neither boast of our own strength, nor that our successors forget that in working out His purposes, God sanctifies even our human infirmities to the fulfillment of His ends."

On October 16, 1847, Rebmann, with the help of eight tribesmen and Bwana Kheri, a caravan leader, set off for the mountain of Kasigau, where they hoped to establish the first mission post. The journey went well and they returned to Mombasa on the 27th of the same month. Along the way they had heard the stories of the great mountain "Kilimansharo," whose head was above the clouds and "topped with silver" and around whose feet lived the mountain's people, the fearsome Jagga (now Chagga).

Krapf immediately sought permission from the governor of Mombasa for an expedition to Jagga land. His official reason was to find areas suitable for mission stations, but the two missionaries were also becoming increasingly interested in the legendary mountain. Disregarding warnings about the "spirits of the mountain," Rebmann and Krapf set off for Jagga on April 27, 1848, and within just two weeks were standing on the great steppe of East Africa within sight of Kilimanjaro. Johann Rebmann was the first European of the modern era to set eyes on the mountain.

In his log, he refers to "a remarkable white on the mountains of Jagga," which he could just make out through the haze. He asked his guide to explain what it was that he was seeing. "He did not know but supposed it to be coldness."[2] At that moment Rebmann realized the legend was true; there were snowfields on the African equator.

On a second expedition in November, Rebmann reached the village of Machame, a point closer to Kilimanjaro than any other European had ever traveled. Here Rebmann was able to accurately describe the shape of the enormous mountain:

> There are two main peaks, which arise from a common base measuring some twenty-five miles long by as many broad. They are separated by a saddle depression, running east and west for a distance of about eight or ten miles. The eastern peak is the lower of the two, and is conical in shape. The western and higher presents the appearance of a magnificent dome, and is covered with snow throughout the year, unlike its eastern neighbor which loses its snowy mantle during the hot season. By the Swahili at the coast, the mountain is known as Kilimanjaro (Mountain of Greatness)

but the Wa-Jagga call it Kibo, from the snow with which it is perpetually capped.[3]

The First Successful Ascent

In August 1887, Professor Hans Meyer, a German geographer, made the first attempt to reach Kibo, the summit of Kilimanjaro. Accompanied by Baron Von Eberstein, Meyer was eventually defeated by a combination of thick snow, large ice walls, and his partner's altitude sickness.

However, Meyer returned the following year traveling with the renowned Alpinist Ludwig Purtscheller and a well-organized support group determined to scale the peak. The climbers came prepared with 19th-century state-of-the-art equipment and established a base camp on the moorland to which porters ferried fresh supplies of food from the village of Marangu.

Daunted by the precipitous ice cliffs at the northern crater rim and extensive ice flows to the south, the two climbers agreed that the best chance of success lay in tackling the less severe incline of the southeastern slope of the mountain. From their advance camp at about 14,000 feet, the two climbers reached the lower slopes of the glacier within a day.

Although the glacier was not as steep or as high as the walls encountered on Meyer's previous attempt, its incline never went below 35 degrees and ice steps had to be cut. Progress was slow. After two hours, the men reached the upper limits of the glacier where the incline decreased. Another two hours of painful trekking through waist-high snow over deep weathered ice grooves found the climbers at the rim of the crater with the summit in sight.

Time and strength were running low and the summit was still another 1,000 feet above, so they returned to their advance camp to try again after three days of rest and recuperation. This time the route was clearly marked and the previously cut ice steps had held their shape. The rim was reached in six hours, and Hans Meyer became the first recorded person to set foot on the highest point in Africa. That evening, Meyer wrote in his journal, "We were in an amiable frame of mind ourselves and, notwithstanding all the toil and trouble my self-appointed task had cost me, I don't think I would that night have changed places with anybody in the world."

Although Meyer and Purtscheller laid the trail for further ascents on Kilimanjaro, there was not an instant queue of would-be climbers. It was a decade before the peak was reached again, and it wasn't until 1912, when a path from Marangu was established and the first huts at Mandera and Horombo were built by Dr. E. Forster for the newly formed German Kilimanjaro Mountain Club, that activity began in earnest. By the early 1930s, hotels in the town of Marangu, at the base of the mountain, began providing a limited number of guided ascents of Kilimanjaro for climbers.

GEOLOGY

Mount Kilimanjaro was born of the catastrophic movements in the earth's crust that created the Great Rift Valley, which runs from the Red Sea through Tanzania to Southern Africa. The Rift Valley is an example of what is known as a constructive margin where new crust is exposed as two continental plates pull away from each other.

At one point, East Africa was a huge flat plain that buckled and ruptured after the African and Eurasian continental plates rebounded off each other causing huge rifting and weak spots in the thinning crust, which led to the formation of many volcanoes in the region. Where the original valley was deepest the volcanic activity was greatest, eventually forming the huge volcanoes of Ngorngoro on the Rift itself and a string of volcanoes to the east, including Mount Meru, Mount Kenya, and Mount Kilimanjaro.

The Rift Valley is still geologically active, and Kilimanjaro is the result of comparatively recent volcanic activity. It originally consisted of three large vents—Shira, Kibo, and Mawenzi. Eventually the Shira cone collapsed and became extinct, followed by Mawenzi. The Kibo cone, however, remained active, spewing forth a massive eruption that released black lava across the Shira Caldera creating the saddle at the base of Mawenzi and forming the ash pit, a crater rim, and the perfect caldera (basin).

Kibo eventually leveled out at just over 19,000 feet and has been periodically covered with ice and glaciers. Around 100,000 years ago a huge landslide created the Barranco Wall on the southwestern edge of the crater. I spent one of the most difficult days of my life on the Barranco Wall, but that will come later.

ECOLOGY

Mount Kilimanjaro is so vast that it generates a microclimate around itself. The rain shadow created to the south and east supplies the beautiful and superbly fertile land in which the towns of Moshi and Arusha are situated. The mountain has five major ecological zones, and the activity within each of these is controlled by the five factors of altitude, rainfall, temperature, flora, and fauna. Each zone occupies an area approximately 3,500 feet in altitude and is subject to a corresponding decrease in rainfall, temperature, and life from the rain forest upward to the summit.

Zone One: Lower Slopes

From the elevation of around 2,500 to 6,000 feet, the slopes of Mount Kilimanjaro are used for food cultivation and the grazing of livestock. The southern lower slopes of Kilimanjaro are filled with human activity. The original scrub and lowland forest have been replaced by grazing land, cultivation, and densely populated settlements fed by water permeating from the forest zone. The land is covered with banana groves and coffee plantations.

The lower slopes were originally earmarked by the British and Germans as potential settlement areas due to the European-like weather. These lush and fertile lands are in stark contrast to the northern slopes, where low rainfall, coupled with the nature of the lava soils, prohibits cultivation. The presence of larger mammals is not frequent in this zone, but smaller tree-dwelling mammals such as Galagos and the tree hyrax are numerous along with the ever elusive genet (a catlike animal). Generally nocturnal, they are usually heard before they are seen.

Zone Two: Forest

A thick rain forest belt, ranging from 6,000 to 9,000 feet, is the richest area on Mount Kilimanjaro. The forest completely encircles the mountain and provides the best conditions for plant life. It serves as the water provider for all the lower slopes, percolating up to 96 percent of all the water on the mountain that originates from this zone, which then percolates down through the porous lava rock to emerge as springs.

The forest supports a variety of wildlife. Occasionally, several large mammals such as elephant or buffalo make their way into the forest. In certain areas, it is compulsory to have an armed guide. From time to time, eland (a genus of antelope) inhabit the border between the forest and the heath and moorland zone. Colobus and blue monkeys are common along with bushbuck, duikers, and an occasional leopard.

Because the forest is damp and high, it generates a daily band of cloud, particularly between 7,500 and 9,000 feet. This cloud promotes high humidity and dampness year round. The daytime average can fluctuate between 60 and 85 degrees. By contrast, the clear nights can produce extremely low temperatures.

Zone Three: Heath and Moorland

Beginning at about 9,000 feet, the forest gives way to the low alpine zone ranging between 9,000 and 13,000 feet. Here, one encounters groves of giant heather reaching up to 30 feet high, dense tussock grass, and abundant and beautiful wildflowers.

Two distinctive plants stand out, *lobelia deckenii* and *senecio kilimanjari*. The *lobelia deckenii* plant is endemic to the area and exceptionally striking. Growing up to 10 feet high, it has a hollow stem, a tall flowerlike spike, and spiraling bracts that conceal blue flowers. In order to protect the sensitive leaf buds from the freezing nighttime temperatures, the *lobelia* close their leaves around the central core while the covered rosettes secrete a slimy solution that helps insulate and preserve.

The *senecio kilimanjari* is a giant groundsel also common in this region. It is one of the most spectacular plants of all. It can reach 15 feet in height with a crown of large leaves and a 3-foot-long spike of yellow flowers. These plants and most of the other vegetation become sparse as the elevation increases and finally fade out completely around 14,750 feet. After this point the terrain becomes truly alpine. This zone does not support abundant wildlife due to its altitude, but there have been sightings of wild dog; buffalo; elephant; and, most commonly, eland.

Zone Four: Highland Desert (Shira Plateau)

The highland desert stretches from 13,000 to 16,500 feet. At this area of the mountain, daytime temperatures range between 32 at dawn and 90 degrees in the mid-day sun. Only the hardiest life survives. At night, the temperature drops well below freezing. We camped at two different points on this broad plateau as we made our way toward the upper regions of the mountain.

Water is scarce and there is little soil to retain what little water there might be. Only 55 recorded plant species survive at this altitude. Lichens and tussock grasses endure in reasonable numbers as do some mosses, but since the soil is subject to movement overnight as the ground water freezes, most root plants find life extremely hard. There are no resident larger animals in the desert, though eland, leopard, and wild dog all pass through on occasion. A few birds can survive in this rarified air and, once again, none are resident. Ravens and several large birds of prey may hunt during the day, but all leave with the sun.

When I reached this region, I began to sense the true expanse of the mountain and the overwhelming feeling of isolation that comes with such a journey. Though it is difficult for plant life to flourish in this region, anxiety takes root easily. Within a few hours on the Shira Plateau, my growing apprehension about the rigors of this climb began to bear the fruit of worry, loneliness, and fear. I became aware that I would, from this time forward, have to conquer two mountains, Kilimanjaro without and a growing struggle with fatigue and doubt within.

Zone Five: The Summit

This region, ranging above 16,500 feet, can best be described as arctic, characterized by freezing cold nights and burning sun during the day where the oxygen level is half that of sea level and there is little to protect the human skin from the sun's radiation. There is negligible liquid surface water because of a combination of low rainfall and porous rock. The bleak terrain supports minimal life forms. What little moisture exists at this altitude is locked up in snow and ice. Lack of water presents a huge obstacle for climbers; one must plan carefully to avoid dehydration at this most critical part of the journey.

Sightings of mammals at this altitude are extremely rare. A frozen leopard was discovered and recorded by the local missionary Dr. Richard Reusch in 1926 and later immortalized by Ernest Hemmingway in his book *The Snows of Kilimanjaro*. No one knows what the leopard was doing at that altitude.

GLACIOLOGY

The summit of Kilimanjaro was previously completely covered by an ice cap more than 350 feet deep, with glaciers ranging well down the mountain to below 13,000 feet. At present, only a small fraction of the glacial cover remains, most visible around the spectacular northern and eastern ice fields and the southern and southwestern flanks. However, the ice is receding at such a rate that there is concern the ice cover may disappear completely within the next 20 years.

DESTINATION

In his book *Across East African Glaciers*, Hans Meyer wrote:
And surely never monarch wore his royal robes more royally than this monarch of African mountains, Kilimanjaro. His foot rests on a carpet of velvety turf, and through

the dark green forest the steps of his throne reach downward to the earth, where man stands awestruck before the glory of his majesty. Art may have colors rich enough to fix one moment of this dazzling splendor, but neither brush nor pen can portray the unceasing play of color—the wondrous purples of the summit deepening as in the Alpine afterglow; the dull greens of the forest and the sepia shadows in the ravines and hollows, growing even darker as evening steals on apace; and last, the gradual fading array of all, as the sun sets, and over everything spreads the grey cloud-curtain of the night. It is not a picture but a pageant—a king goes to his rest.[4]

It is to this mountain of history and mystery that I travel. My trip will take me by air from Chicago to Amsterdam and then on to Tanzania. Although I have researched the journey carefully and have been preparing for several months, I know there is a fundamental difference between armchair travel and the real thing.

I can imagine what it might be like to hoist a large backpack and set off on a climb into the sky, but only time will tell for sure what awaits me on the other side of the world. It is not just a journey of latitude and longitude but one of altitude as well. This will surely be a trip of introspection and testing, for I expect to learn much about both the mountain and the climber.

I am well aware that making it to the summit is far from being a sure thing. More than 60 percent of those who attempt this climb have to turn back. Only a very few stand at the summit and look down on the clouds that shelter the vast plains. Soon I will see if I have what it takes to reach the top of the mountain. Either way, it will be all right. I do not hesitate for fear of failure. To make the attempt is to succeed already—the only thing in question now is what kind of success awaits. Time will tell my story.

2
READY, SET, GO

All that we do is done with an eye to something else.
—Aristotle

When I was a kid, the playground mantra was, "Ready, set, go!" Going followed getting everything ready. The race at camp or at school could never start until the counselor or coach made sure everyone was ready and all the arrangements were set. From the day I first got the idea of climbing the mountain, I was well aware that my chances for success, my safety, and the enjoyment of the trip would be impacted by the level and thoroughness of my preparation.

I organized my preparation into four quadrants: logistics, equipment, physical training, and mental/spiritual preparation.

LOGISTICS

The government of Tanzania requires everyone who attempts to climb Kilimanjaro to go with an approved guide and follow a generally prescribed route. So one of the first things a person must do is to research available guides. It is possible to just show up in Tanzania and make contact with a climbing company, but for many reasons it is much better to do adequate research ahead of time so that a guide and outfitter can be secured well in advance.

My sources of information were guidebooks (see the bibliography) and the Internet. Entering "climbing Mt. Kilimanjaro" into a Web-based search engine yielded 44,833 responses. These sites provide all a person needs to know and much, much more. As I surfed the Net, I began to read testimonials and online journals posted by those who had made the climb. This source gave me a nonfiltered look at what such an undertaking was really like. I also found Web pages for various outfitters and tour companies. Most of the companies specialized in safaris; but little by little I began to make a list of the ones that also assisted individuals who wished to climb Kilimanjaro. Carefully reviewing these pages, I began to narrow the list to those companies that seemed most reliable.

I also discovered through the Net that there is an IMAX film, *Kilimanjaro: To the Roof of Africa.* I ordered a copy. Once I watched the DVD, I began to believe in earnest that this was something I could do if I took sufficient time and care to prepare. I observed that the IMAX team of climbers and camera crew were taken to the summit under the direction of Thomson Safaris. I located the Thomson Web site and began to carefully review this company's services. I then contacted them for more information and received a detailed letter outlining the process for arranging such a climb.

I reviewed the options available through Thomson, then called and talked to a staff member in their U.S. office in Boston. After receiving my reservation deposit, Thomson sent me a helpful booklet called *The Trekker's Preparation Guide.* It contained, in about 25 pages, everything I needed to know to get ready for the climb.

A person can climb Kilimanjaro at any time of the year, but the best overall weather conditions are in January. That was a good time for me as well, so I settled on a climb scheduled from January 20 to February 1, on the rigorous Western Breach route. I then got busy booking my airline flights. The preferred option proved to be a KLM flight from Chicago to Tanzania, via Amsterdam. I bought my tickets and thought, "Am I really going through with this?"

In addition to a U.S. passport, visitors to Tanzania must obtain a visa to enter the country. Although a person can obtain a visa upon arrival in Tanzania, it's better to get that paperwork completed long before his or her departure. I completed an application form in November and sent it, along with my passport, two photos, and a certified check for $50.00 to the Tanzania Embassy in Washington. I am always leery of sending my passport anywhere, but since the visa had to be stamped directly into the passport, I had little choice. The process went smoothly and my passport with the visa returned to me within two weeks.

HEALTH PREPARATIONS

Staying healthy throughout the climb begins by being as healthy as possible when arriving in Africa. The guidebook from Thomson reminded me, "No one with a sore throat, cold, or with breathing problems should go above 10,000 feet." A few months before leaving, I consulted my family physician and reviewed the trip with him. He updated my general physical exam and ordered an EKG and stress test from a cardiologist. I was also given the name of a fine travel and immunization clinic at Northwestern University Hospital in Chicago. This clinic specializes in the health requirements of travelers, particularly those visiting third world areas.

The physician at the clinic reviewed my proposed itinerary and checked the latest information from the U.S. State Department and Centers for Disease Control for travel advisories. She then recommended a regimen of five inoculations and four prescriptions. Over the next few weeks, I received vaccinations for yellow fever, diphtheria-tetanus, polio, typhoid, and a booster for hepatitis. I was given a prescription for Larium to combat malaria, which I was to begin taking two weeks prior to my departure and for a period of four weeks following my return. I also received prescriptions for Ciprofloxacin—a general antibiotic to be used as needed—and for an antidiarrhea medication.

The doctor then asked if I had considered taking Diamox, which is taken by some climbers to help combat altitude sickness. I had read about it extensively. "I know about it, but have not been planning to use it because of the side effects," I told her.

"Well, I have given it to several others and they have not had a problem. You may want to take it along, in case you decide you want to try it," she replied.

I agreed to do so. At the very least I would get the prescription filled and take the pills to Africa. This drug helps the respiratory system maintain fluid in the lungs and head at high altitudes. It enables a person to breathe more often so that he or she can take in more oxygen. Little did I know that I would pay a significant price for this decision once the trip began. But at this point I felt if Diamox could improve my chances, even slightly, I should take it.

In addition to the prescriptions, I prepared a personal first-aid kit, which included bandages, safety pins, scissors, ibuprofen, moleskin (for blisters), a plastic thermometer, sunblock and lip balm, antibiotic cream (Neosporin), insect repellent, and antiseptic wipes.

Since there is no potable water available once the climb begins, climbers must bring filters and chemical treatments. Many microorganisms can be removed from water by straining or pumping it through a compact, lightweight filter system. But although filters remove organisms and suspended solids from water, they do not chemically treat the water for microscopic contaminants. The remaining water-borne organisms can be rendered inactive by adding iodine or chlorine dioxide to the filtered water. So, in preparation, I purchased a small hand pump filtering system and a supply of high-potency iodine tablets. I made sure to test the pump before leaving the United States. It would be disastrous to discover a malfunction once I was on the mountain.

I wanted to give myself the best chance to reach the summit, so I had chosen a first-rate company to guide me and selected a longer route, which was more difficult in some ways but allowed for more acclimatization time. Adjusting to the extremely high altitude was considered by many to be the single biggest obstacle to reaching the summit. I also chose the best time of the year to climb. All through my preparation, I was committed to doing everything I could to increase my chances of success. My next step was to map out a rigorous training program and begin assembling the right clothing and equipment.

EQUIPMENT AND SUPPLIES

A climber's equipment is very important and can significantly affect his or her chance of succeeding on the mountain. He or she must be prepared for all eventualities and have sufficient resources to combat extremes of temperature, exposure, and weather.

Little by little I accumulated what I would need. My clothing, equipment, and supplies included the following:

Clothing

- Gore-Tex shell (for the upper body; a waterproof/breathable shell with a hood, which I supplemented with layering underneath allowing for perspiration to escape and giving me the flexibility to add or shed layers as climatic conditions changed)
- Gore-Tex rain pants (to be worn over long underwear and/or fleece pants)

- Two pair of loose-fitting synthetic pants, one of which was convertible into shorts for the early part of the climb and the last day of descent
- Hiking shorts
- Fleece pants (Jeans are not good for hiking; they are heavy and cold when wet.)
- Heavyweight fleece jacket
- Lightweight long-sleeve sweater
- Lightweight long-sleeve synthetic shirts
- Baseball-style cap
- Rain poncho
- Fleece hat that covers the ears
- One lightweight and one heavyweight pair of gloves
- Balaclava face protection
- Bandanas
- Lightweight synthetic briefs
- Lightweight thermal long underwear—top and bottom
- Synthetic T-shirts
- Hiking boots (This is perhaps the single most important piece of equipment. They must be waterproof, highly durable, with at least a three-quarter-length shank. I chose a pair of Asolo TPS 520 GTX boots. They were excellent!)
- A simple lightweight pair of trail shoes for changing into at the end of a trekking day
- Several pair of sturdy hiking socks

Equipment
- Sleeping bag (rated for subfreezing conditions)
- Sleeping pad or ground mat
- Three one-liter capacity wide-mouth plastic water bottles (two for drinking, one for urine)
- Gaiters (These wrap around a climber's shoes and legs to the knees. This is a very sound investment. The early

stages of the climb can be exceptionally muddy, and the use of gaiters helps to keep feet dry and prevent blisters and fungus. On the higher stretches of the mountain, scree and gravel are everywhere. Gaiters help stop small shards of lava and rock from getting inside a climber's footwear.)

- Trekking poles (These poles are very useful when ascending and even more helpful when descending steep terrain and/or scree-covered slopes. The poles provide extra balance and help support a climber's weight, taking the pressure off the knees.)
- Whistle
- Flashlight
- Headlight
- Extra batteries
- Mountaineering sunglasses
- Waterproof stuff sacks
- Towel and washcloth
- Plastic zip-lock bags
- Money belt
- Camera and film

All clothing, equipment, and supplies were to be divided into two bags: a backpack carried (worn) by the climber and a duffle or rucksack to be carried by a porter. There is a strict weight limit for the bag to be carried by the porter. It cannot weigh more than 33 pounds. The backpack worn by the climber generally weighs between 15 and 20 pounds.

I found it very difficult to stay under these weight limits even by taking the minimum. Once in Africa, I ended up leaving my heavier coat, my second pair of shoes, and some miscellaneous items in my travel bag at the base of the mountain in order to meet these weight regulations.

CONDITIONING

I decided I would need to drop 10 pounds before the climb and increase my overall level of fitness and endurance. I began some basic conditioning about six months prior to the climb and started a detailed training program four months before going.

My first priority was to build my endurance and tone my muscles so that I could walk 5 to 10 miles a day for six or seven days in a row while carrying a 15-pound backpack. Fortunately, I live on a university campus with a mile-long outdoor walking track and near a large hiking and recreational area called Perry Farm. Although my schedule did not allow me to work out every day, I was able to walk at least three days a week.

I began with two miles a day and then added a mile a day each week so that by the end of six weeks I was able to hike five to eight miles a day without much difficulty. In addition to developing endurance and strengthening leg muscles, the physical training was also designed to help me prepare mentally. It is difficult to suddenly go from a crowded, people-filled life to long expanses of solitude. My training hikes helped me prepare for extended times of isolation.

MENTAL PREPARATION

Being ready mentally is nearly as important as physical conditioning. A large part of a climb is dependent upon a climber's ability to stay focused. There are times when the trip is particularly grueling and other times when monotony sets in. Training for an extended period helped me adjust to this tedium. Doing a series of long walks for several weeks not only tones a person physically but sharpens his or her mental focus as well.

Mental toughness is more than just a matter of will. It also requires conditioning, including learning how to keep going once fatigue and/or boredom sets in. A higher level of self-discipline developed as I made myself change into my climbing clothes and set out for a long hike before work in the morning, on a Saturday, or at the end of the day during the week.

A close cousin of mental strength is emotional balance. Emotional strength and stability are also important in an undertaking such as this. Emotionally, a person must be able to stay positive even in the face of fatigue or strain. Mood swings deplete energy and erode focus. One thing I began to do as I prepared was to memorize passages from the Psalms. I identified a series of psalms that spoke specifically about the wonders of nature and started committing those to memory as I trained. This not only helped with the boredom that can easily set in but also filled my mind with the nourishment of the Word. Later, this was to help guard and stabilize my feelings as I spent hours walking, seemingly, to nowhere.

Because of this practice, I decided that the only written material I would take with me would be a copy of the Psalms. I expanded my reading through the Psalms during the weeks of training, giving attention to passages I thought might be particularly helpful once I was on the mountain.

For me there was a strong spiritual component to the trip, so I also spent time in spiritual preparation prior to my departure. This included times of prayer and reflection. In addition to my life in the Psalms, I began to read those passages in the Bible that spoke of times alone. I noted how often Jesus would withdraw from the crowds, including His 40 days in the wilderness just prior to His public ministry.

Prepared for Danger

On January 6, two weeks to the day before my departure, the following story appeared on page 7 of the *Chicago Tribune*. I just happened to see it as I was having breakfast with some friends at a local restaurant.

TANZANIA: 3 American climbers killed in Mt. Kilimanjaro rock slide

> KILIMANJARO NATIONAL PARK—*Three Americans
> were killed and two others seriously injured when boulders
> rained down on climbers as they slept before a predawn ascent
> of Africa's highest peak. The Americans were . . . camped near
> Arrow Glacier on Mt. Kilimanjaro's difficult Western Breach
> when the rockslide occurred Wednesday.*

I was stunned. I just couldn't believe what I was reading. This tragic accident happened on the very route I would be taking. From the *Tribune* story and other news reports, which I pulled from the Internet later that day, it seemed that a sudden change in weather at the peak had dislodged the rocks that tumbled down onto the sleeping climbers below.

Suddenly the danger ever lurking in the background of my thinking and planning was front and center. Should I reconsider? Dare I even mention this to my wife, Jill? I thought about it throughout the day and decided I would still make the trip. It also seemed only right to let Jill read the articles as well.

As we talked about the articles, I assured her I would be as careful as I could be. We joked about how the trip to the airport in Chicago traffic might be the most dangerous part of the journey. The death of the other climbers reminded me that in spite of all the preparation a person might make for such a trip, life itself is unpredictable and the world is a dangerous place. This is true, yet we need not be paralyzed by what *could* happen and miss what *can* happen amid the adventure of life itself.

Even faced with the inherent dangers of such a climb, I was, nonetheless, drawn to this mountain by its majesty and mystery. Neville Shulman, author of *On Top of Africa*, writes, "Kilimanjaro is one of the great mountains of the world. Anyone who reaches its summit has achieved no mean feat . . . to stand on the roof of Africa you will experience the kind of exhilaration which comes but rarely in any individual's lifetime."[5]

3

THE JOURNEY BEGINS

Most men pursue pleasure with such breathless haste
they often hurry past it.
—Søren Kierkegaard

Overnight: KLM Flight 612, Seat 22c (39,000 feet)

Friday, January 20

Today started early—up at 5:20 A.M., breakfast at Blues Café on Station Street—one pancake with crisp bacon. It was a rather ordinary beginning for what should prove to be an extraordinary journey.

Many days, most of them in fact, which end up as extraordinary, begin as ordinary days—some good, some difficult. I remember the day I was elected president of the university where I serve. The day was ordinary in nearly every respect, until my phone rang late that night. I was awakened from a sound sleep by a call from the chairman of the Board of Trustees. "Dr. Bowling, I am calling to tell you that you have just been elected as the 12th president of Olivet Nazarene University."

What had been an ordinary day was changed in a moment, a wonderful moment. My life from that day forward would be different. Such is the difference one day can make in a person's life.

By contrast, I was up early one day last fall, preparing for a trip to Boston, when I received a call that my father was desperately ill. Within the hour I was speeding across the Midwest toward a distant hospital. My plans were suddenly superseded, set aside, by the circumstances of life and the providence of God.

Ordinary days have a way of becoming extraordinary for good or ill. Keeping one's balance, as a person navigates the journey from ordinary to extraordinary and back again, brings both challenge and energy to life. Who knows when an ordinary moment, an ordinary day, or an ordinary life may be transformed in an instant to something quite extraordinary.

Last night at about nine o'clock the doorbell rang and I opened the door to find about 15 university students standing in the cold with a sign, Bon Voyage! I invited them in for a few minutes. It was a very nice moment, for although I hadn't been aware of it, my anxiety level about this adventure had begun to rise significantly as I realized I would be leaving on the coming day and that, one way or the other, this trip would change my life. One of the fellows jokingly volunteered to watch my car while I was gone. The others assured me they would be thinking and praying for me every day until I returned.

After the students left, I finished packing and crawled into bed at 10:30 P.M. I lay there for a moment thinking that clean sheets, a comfortable bed, and the warmth of an electric blanket on a cold winter night would soon give way to a tiny tent, a sleeping bag, and a backpack for a pillow.

Following my breakfast at Blues this morning, I attended a bank board meeting and then stopped by the office for about 30 minutes before heading home to change for the trip. Jill said she would meet me at the airport when I got back, but she didn't want to take me to the airport: "If you leave from the house and I am still here, it will seem like just another trip. But if I have to pull away from the airport and drive home alone, the realization that this is not just another trip will be more than I want to deal with."

So my friend Ray Bellomy picked me up right at noon for the trip to the airport. Jill and I said good-bye at the garage door as we had done a hundred times before. "See you when I get back," I said, realizing I would have absolutely no contact with her again until I returned to America in two weeks. We both knew there was a strong measure of uncertainty about what the next two weeks would hold for both of us. What unforeseen events were about to unfold?

"Let's circle the campus on our way out of town," I said to Ray. I wanted to see it all before I left. It was now 12:15 P.M. We didn't talk much on the way to Chicago. I had already started narrowing my focus, and there wasn't much room for small talk. We arrived at O'Hare International Airport in good time. I checked in at the KLM counter and made my way through the labyrinth of security measures. Once inside the boarding area, I sat down to eat a quick late lunch and begin writing these lines in my travel journal.

Journal: *O'Hare International Airport, Chicago (2:38 P.M.)*

It is so cold outside that it is cold inside here at the airport as well. The temperature reading on the car when I unloaded my bags was 13 degrees. It is hard to believe that I will soon be at the equator, sleeping under the stars.

In an hour or so I will depart on KLM flight 612 to Amsterdam. This will be the first leg of what, no doubt, will prove to be an extraordinary journey. The flight of 4,109 miles will take seven and one-half hours. I am scheduled to arrive at 7 A.M. tomorrow morning.

I am surrounded by scores of people and yet I am alone, really alone. It is so interesting to sit for a time in the midst of a busy international terminal at a major airport. You can travel the world while sitting still. The landscape of the globe and the map of history come walking by in the faces, voices, and appearance of passengers from nearly every nation on earth.

The staff has just announced the flight. My boarding pass is now in my hand. The Jetway door stands as a sentinel before me, guarding my next step. My mind is filled with anticipation, but there is a fair measure of anxiety as well. The next two weeks will bring daily challenges—physical, mental, and emotional.

Got to go . . .

Onboard KLM Flight 612 to Amsterdam

As I settle into my seat, I take a deep breath. I am relatively calm as I think about the adventure just ahead. I have made good preparation, even though I am sure I could have trained harder physically. Time will tell. The logistical preparation seems to have all gone well. I have good equipment, a climbing schedule that will give me an excellent chance to make it to the summit, and my mental focus is strong and steady.

It is interesting how such a trip expands and at the same time narrows one's focus. I will cross the globe and look into the eyes of people from many countries on earth. I will rub shoulders and sit beside men and women who live vastly different lives—and yet, I will speak to very few of these folks. I will see sights that are broad and expansive but sleep alone in a small tent.

I suppose living is always a balance between a person's interior being and his or her physical and social surroundings. There is a tension there but not necessarily in a negative way. Rather, like a violin that makes no music until the strings are stretched, a certain amount of tension fine-tunes a person's daily life.

This trip, the challenge of the climb itself, the reflection at the end of the day, the interaction with my fellow climbers, and my time alone with God will take me out of myself. All of these things will stretch the strings of my life—physically, mentally, socially, and spiritually. I wonder what new music will follow.

The one question I have wrestled with is this, "Why am I making this climb?" Is it an expression of a delayed midlife crisis? I have some ideas as to the why, but I am not sure I fully understand it myself. I am content to not wonder too much about the why. I am at ease to wait and see what the experience means to me as I climb, confident there are lessons to learn that will enrich my life.

Jill gave me a scripture reference for the trip from Ps. 95, "For the LORD is the great God, the great King above all gods. In his hand are the depths of the earth, and the mountain peaks belong to him" (vv. 3-4). If one applies this passage broadly, it suggests that God is there in the low points of life and also at the peaks.

Living in a busy, noisy world can lead to losing a keen awareness of the nearness of God. My sense is that living closer to nature—feeling the wind, sun, and rain; sleeping under the stars; watching the sun rise and set—helps tune one's physical and spiritual senses.

There are times when what we look for (long for) is with us all the time, we just don't know it. "Many search for happiness as we look for a hat we are wearing on our heads."[6] So what does it take to notice something that is very near, that we are looking for but do not see?

Perhaps first, we should stop looking, sit for a time, and lay aside the search. Let it come to us. This may be why I am not obsessed with why I am making this climb. I am not going because I am searching for something that is missing in my life. I am going simply to go; to leave the ordinary life behind so that I might experience the extraordinary.

At the same time, extraordinary doesn't always mean extra ordinary. I am not just playing with words; some great insights and experiences come in very subtle, simple ways. I am reminded that God did not appear to Elijah in the fire or the wind but in a still, small voice.

Leaving behind the banter and volume of daily 21st-century life to seek a quieter voice, I travel to a place of solitude inhabited only by wind and light and shadow. I seek a rhythm not made by men and anticipate a kind of luxury-of-want waiting on the mountain.

The flight seems to be completely filled. It amazes me each time I am on such a flight just how many people crisscross continents and countries every day. For this particular flight, I am on a Boeing 747 that holds 440 people. Fortunately, I am on an aisle seat, which allows a little more room and easy access to get up and walk around. I have decided to skip the meal, forego the in-flight entertainment, close my eyes, offer a prayer, and spend my first night sleeping at 39,000 feet.

Every journey begins with one step and the real challenge of attaining any goal is to begin—begin with the end in mind. I am glad to be on my way. As I sit quietly, I think only of standing on the summit, stepping onto the roof of Africa, looking out across a continent. What will it be like to journey by foot above the clouds?

The engines hum and the cabin lights are dimmed; I am aware that Mount Kilimanjaro awaits me. I feel certain that my perspective will change concerning the physical world and the revelation of God it provides. But there will also be a change of inner perspective as well. Will I see my life differently once I've been to the mountain?

PRAYER

Dear God, the adventure has begun. I am unsure of many things; but, nonetheless, I am sure of You. I do not know what tomorrow will bring, but I know that You will be there with me and that is sufficient. Watch over me and all who fly tonight. Guide my steps as I journey. Guard my heart and mind as well. Holy Spirit, be my Teacher; let me hear Your voice in the wind and in the stillness. Let me see Your hand in the beauty and majesty of the mountain. I open myself to the lessons You will teach me. Amen.

4

OUT TO AFRICA

It is not the mountain we conquer, but ourselves.
—Hans Meyer

Overnight: KIA Lodge—Arusha, Tanzania (4,451 feet)

Journal: *Saturday, January 21, 7:50 A.M.*

The flight from the United States arrived in Amsterdam about 20 minutes early. We deplaned right next to the gate from which I will depart for East Africa. The trip last night was peaceful, and I was able to sleep most of the way. Having finished a walk through the terminal—very modern, lots of shops, restaurants, a hotel, and a casino—I grab a quick breakfast, quiche and coffee. I also notice a place where travelers can take a shower, change clothes, and freshen up. I take note; this may come in handy on the way home.

It is still a little hard to believe that I will be in tropical East Africa tonight. It also seems a little odd to be traveling alone. That is unusual for me. It reminds me of a long trip from Calcutta back to the United States, which I made a few years ago. Late one afternoon, John Anderson, a veteran retired missionary who accompanied me on that journey, and I parted after spending a month together making our way around India. From time to time during that trip, when we found ourselves in an odd place or a strange situation, John would say to me, "It's a long way from Bourbonnais" (our hometown). I am pretty sure I will feel that way tonight.

As I sit now in the departure area for the flight to Tanzania, I am taken by the array of people assembling for this flight. The passengers on the flight from Chicago to Amsterdam were pretty generic, North Americans and northern Europeans. Not so on this flight.

It is, naturally, a smaller plane and the passengers now appear to represent a wide array of nationalities. There are a handful other Americans—I heard them before I saw them—and some European businessmen, but not in suits and ties. There are several individuals from India and, of course, a number of Africans.

I think I'll never tire of looking at faces. Each face tells a story, reveals a legacy, and has a way of saying either yes or no to all who gaze upon it. In one set of eyes, there is power; in another, the gaze is shy. A child's face is all mirth, unrestrained smiles and uninhibited delight. Occasionally there is sadness seeping from a face. On others there is tense anxiety.

Five rather rough-looking men have entered the gate area, carrying backpacks. Are they climbers? If so, I hope they are with another group. The thought of making the climb with the Hell's Angels is not very appealing. We'll see . . .

It seems odd that airlines often name their planes. British Airways does this, and I just noticed that KLM, my airline for this trip, does the same. The plane we're flying to Africa is the Audrey Hepburn. She didn't die in a plane crash, did she?

As the parade of passengers passes, I notice how folks are dressed for travel. Things have changed. The first time I flew, I was in the fifth grade. My older brother, Michael, and I flew from Dayton, Ohio, to Cleveland by ourselves. We were going to visit our cousins, and my parents thought it would be a good experience for us to fly. Not many people traveled by air in those days. Our flight was on a TWA twin-engine propeller plane, which only flew at about 10,000 feet.

For this trip, Mom dressed us in suits and ties. We must have looked like two miniature executives on a business trip. In those days, however, people dressed up for such occasions. If we wore suits for such a short flight from Dayton to Cleveland, I am sure we would have been in tuxedos for a flight to Europe. That is not the case today. Anything will do. Comfort rules. I can't quite believe that some of the individuals I have seen this morning stood in front of a mirror earlier today and said to themselves, "This is how I want to present myself to the world today." But who knows, they may be saying the same thing about me!

Onboard, 10:38 A.M.

I have just boarded KLM flight 571 from Amsterdam to Kilimanjaro International Airport, near the town of Arusha, Tanzania. This flight will take another eight and a half hours. I am a little more restless than I was yesterday as I find my seat, because I know that when this plane touches down, I will be in Africa—no turning back. I intend to alternate between sitting, standing, and walking about during the flight, along with some time for some additional sleep—there will be plenty of time for all of this. We take off right on time.

3:23 P.M.

Surely we must be almost halfway there. I've been sleeping off and on for the last couple of hours and now I walk to the back of the plane to stand for a while just as our flight crosses the African coastal line. The deep blue of the southern Mediterranean suddenly gives way to the pale tan of the Sahara Desert. What a vast and foreboding place. The day is clear, so I can see the ground easily, but there is nothing there—absolutely nothing. There are no towns, no roads, no rivers or trees or any sign of life, just barren land, a vast monochrome surface stretching out in all directions. This adds to my growing feeling of isolation.

We are above Egypt, the land of the pharaohs and the great pyramids. We travel at 39,000 feet across the desert of southwestern Egypt, pass into Sudan, flying over Khartoum, then across Ethiopia. The sun sets over East Africa as we cross the border into Kenya and draw close to crossing the equator as we start the last leg of this flight.

8 P.M.

We are now about 40 minutes from touchdown. The view outside is darkness, which means I won't get to see Kilimanjaro until tomorrow morning. I had been hoping that we might get close enough to catch a glimpse of it from the air; but I guess I will see enough of the mountain in the days to come. I am certainly developing a heightened sense of adventure as we get close. "I just want to live while I'm alive," is a phrase playing in my ears right now over the KLM audio system. Prophetic?

In the Amsterdam airport, earlier today, I noticed a saying printed on the back of a young man's T-shirt. It read, "The journey is the destination." Good thought for today, and perhaps every day.

Fasten seat belts, trays up, seats in place, we are landing.

Stepping out of the plane and making my way down the stairs onto the tarmac, I immediately feel the warm African breeze. It is 8:47 P.M. A few steps before me I see a small, underlit, single-story terminal building. It is the KJO International Airport in northeastern Tanzania. Because we have landed in the dark, I do not have a sense of the typography of the area. The airport is a potpourri of sights, sounds, and smells—all of which announce to my senses, "You are now in Africa."

My first stop in the terminal is the immigration desk. I hand my passport to a young man who is neatly dressed in a military uniform. He leafs through the pages slowly, then stops to carefully review the Tanzanian visa stamped into the document.

"How long will you be here?" he asks politely, without looking up.

"About two weeks," I reply.

"The purpose of your trip?" he inquires, now looking straight into my eyes.

At this point time stands still and several responses race through my mind. For some reason, I don't feel comfortable saying, "I've come to climb Mount Kilimanjaro." I think I am subconsciously uneasy tackling such an obstacle at my age. While I had no problem talking about it at home, I realize this man knows the mountain, has seen would-be climbers come and go for years, and might very well take one look at me and reply, "No, seriously, what brings you to East Africa?"

With all of that flashing before me in an instant, I simply reply, "I am here on a holiday." I would later come to realize what a misstatement that was! But it satisfied the officer who stamped my passport and said, "*Asante*," to which I replied, "*Asante sana.*" This brief exchange—"Thank you" and "Thank you very much"—was my first in Swahili.

Swahili is the official and most common language of Tanzania. It is spoken widely throughout East Africa. The language originated as part of the trading culture of Zanzibar and the east coast. It is a Bantu language with various Arab influences. I have learned that although many people in East Africa speak English, using even a little Swahili builds a more personal bond with the indigenous people.

Perhaps the most common Swahili phrase now in use in the United States is *hakuna matata*, which means "no problem." It was popularized by the Broadway musical and the movie *The Lion King*. Other simple phrases are:

jambo (good morning or hello)

habari gani? (how are you?)

karibu (welcome)

ndiyo (yes)

hapana (no)

kahawa (coffee)

Phrases that I am sure we will hear once we are on the mountain are *twendai* (let's go!) and *pole, pole* (slowly, slowly).

I step through large double doors into a chaotic baggage area. It is crucial that my gray duffle bag has made it from Chicago. It would be almost impossible to make the climb without that bag. I have packed the bare essentials into my backpack, which I've used as a carry-on; but I doubt I could replace the other items in my gray duffle in time to make the climb as planned.

The room is crowded and hot. There is only one large carousel for luggage, but it is not yet moving. While waiting, I scan the faces milling about—are any of these folks among my climbing partners? Suddenly, the carousel jerks its way to life and ever so slowly the bags from our flight begin to appear. Within a few minutes I see my bag. Relief!

I now make my way to clear customs. A handful of armed officials stand talking behind a table.

"Where are you from?" one of the officials asks me.

"The United States."

Without comment or expression I am waved through. It seems I could have had an elephant in my bag and they wouldn't be concerned.

Once I am through customs, I step outside the restricted area into a large open-air arrival hall hoping that someone will be there to meet me. Sure enough, there is a young man with a professionally lettered sign that reads "Thomson," the name of the company providing the guide and support staff. As I approach him, I am greeted with a gleaming smile and a warm welcoming handshake.

"My name is Thomas," he says. "What's yours?"

I give him my name and he checks it against a small list attached to his clipboard. "Now we are to meet three others," he tells me.

Within a moment or two a tall, thin fellow approaches us and says his name is Vince.

"Two more," Thomas says, eyeing his list.

"Hello, Vince, my name is John. Are you doing the climb?"

"Yes, you too?"

I nod.

"I have a friend who did this climb last year. He said it was great."

"Did he make it all the way to the top?" I ask.

"Yes, but he told me the hardest part was coming down."

"I have heard that is the most difficult; but I think if I can make it to the summit, I will be so glad to be headed down, that, as hard as it may be, I'll be able to make it."

Just then a third climber joins us. His name is Leo and he is from Portland, Maine. He appears to be just a few years younger than I. Although he doesn't look like a climber, there is an air of confidence about him. I am struck immediately by his winsome, broad smile. I like him right away. And then Scott appears. Scott is an attorney from Hartford, Connecticut. He has a friendly, yet determined manner. "He is serious about this climb," I think to myself as I study his face and manner.

Thomas motions for the four of us to follow him. We put on our backpacks, grab our duffle bags, and head out to a parking area. "I am not your guide," Thomas says, in response to a question from Leo. "But I will take you to where you are staying tonight. You will meet your guides and the other climbers in the morning."

We hoist our large bags onto the roof of his vehicle, throw a tarp on top, and strap them down. "We're not going far," Thomas tells us as we climb inside. He drives slowly out of the airport and onto a small paved road. What strikes me immediately is how very dark it is. There are no lights on the road and only a few lights scattered about in the distance.

After only about 10 minutes, we leave the pavement for a dirt road with deep potholes; Thomas slows the vehicle to a crawl. We lurch forward and backward and from side to side as our tires sink and then emerge from the holes. "We call this an African massage," Thomas says. We laugh a bit but cannot help but quietly wonder what kind of hotel could be at the end of such a dark and desolate road.

I must admit that I had pretty low expectations for where we might spend this first night, but to my delight the KIA Lodge is quite nice. We enter a small, bright, open-air reception area. Several staff members dressed in traditional African attire greet us with a friendly, "Jambo" (hello). We are given moist hand towels and a glass of juice (passion fruit, I think) as we present our passports for check-in.

Once assigned a room, a porter grabs my bag, bows slightly, and says, "Follow me, please." The accommodations consist of private little bungalows that stand along a serpentine pathway lined with tropical plants, flowers, and trees. The air is fragrant with the scent of the vast Serengeti plain that surrounds us for hundreds of miles, and there is a strong fragrance of bougainvilleas.

I am led to number 27. The room is large and comfortably furnished. As we turn on the light, I see only one or two resident visitors dart across the floor into the shadows. I hand the porter a few Tanzanian shillings and thank him for his service and hospitality. A packet of documents was waiting for me when I checked in. Among the contents is a schedule for tomorrow. Following breakfast there is to be an initial meeting with our guides and then we will be transferred to a campsite on the far western side of the mountain.

I realize I am tired and yet restless at the same time. I take a few minutes to inspect my luggage, making sure everything is still there. Then I decide to repack for the climb. I also fill a small travel bag, which had been loaded into the duffle, to leave at the hotel. It contains my clothes for the trip home and a few other things not absolutely necessary for the climb.

After an hour or so, I shower and crawl into bed. As I lay there, far from home on the eve of a great adventure, surrounded by mosquito nets, beneath the spinning blades of a large ceiling fan, I thank the Lord for His presence and His traveling mercies. It is 11:15 P.M. in Africa, 4:15 in the afternoon at home, and my body is somewhere in between.

PRAYER

Now I lay me down to sleep . . . Lord, I thank You for being with me on this journey. I know that You are always with me and that You are present everywhere. I recall the words of the psalmist:

> *Where can I go from your Spirit?*
>   *Where can I flee from your presence?*
> *If I go up to the heavens, you are there;*
>   *if I make my bed in the depths, you are there.*
> *If I rise on the wings of the dawn,*
>   *if I settle on the far side of the sea,*
> *even there your hand will guide me,*
>   *your right hand will hold me fast.*
>
> —Ps. 139:7-10

Here I am "on the far side of the sea." I know You are here with me and I will rest in Your presence tonight. Amen.

5
ANTICIPATION INTENSIFIES

Every now and again take a good look at something not made with hands—a mountain, a star, the turn of a stream. There will come to you wisdom and patience and solace and, above all, the assurance that you are not alone in the world.
—Sidney Lovett

Overnight: Ndarakwai Camp, West Kilimanjaro (5,280 feet)

I will use today to recover from the long flight and begin the cultural adjustments required by such a trip. This morning consists of a climb briefing at the lodge before transferring to our base camp on the west side of Kilimanjaro.

There are few mountains in the world whose name evokes as much wonder and awe. Kilimanjaro holds a unique place in both the western and African psyche. Kili (the shorthand name of the mountain) is a complex mountain consisting of three separate extinct volcanic peaks: Kibo (19,341 feet), Mawenzi (16,893 feet), and Shira (at 12,999 feet). To confuse matters, the summit of Kilimanjaro is called both Kibo and Uhuru Peak.

In 1973, Mount Kilimanjaro was designated a Tanzanian national park. This was done to help preserve the wilderness environment of the mountain and control the number of climbers. All visitors, as I had learned earlier, are required to travel with a registered guide anytime they go inside the park boundaries, even if it is for a short one-day hike.

Journal: *Sunday, January 22*

I did not sleep well—jet lag, I think. It's now morning and a golden African glow seeps into my room. I shower, dress, and go outside for a walk along the path that winds toward the main building. It is already hot; what a contrast to the freezing cold of January in Chicago. The path I am walking meanders in a gentle way. I like that. It suggests a slower pace; no hurry, take your time. Smell the flowers. The lodge is just outside of the town of Arusha in a stunning location with a magnificent view of the mountain.

7:45 A.M.

I am the first to arrive for breakfast, what a beautiful setting. The staff has prepared a full buffet including a nice array of fresh fruits, cereals, meats, cheeses, and breads. Eggs are cooked to order.

Leo and Vince show up next, cameras in hand. As we sit together for a moment, drinking our strong African coffee, the other members of our group begin to join us for breakfast.

"Hi, my name is Tim and this is Carey. Are you guys with Thomson?"

We say we are and introduce ourselves. Tim and Carey LeRoux are an energetic young couple from midtown Manhattan. Tim manages a bond fund, and Carey is an attorney. Scott arrives next, followed by a young man named Christian. Christian is a civilian employee at the U.S. Military Academy at West Point. He is young and fit. He seems a little nervous as we gather.

The setting brings to mind a scene from one of those plays that gathers an odd assortment of people in a remote hotel to await some unexpected event. At first we are not quite ourselves; we are on edge. We are talkative and yet quiet at the same time. Here we are, after months of preparation, about to climb the highest mountain in Africa, something we have never attempted before, with no guarantee that we will succeed.

As far as we can tell, the seven of us will comprise our climbing group—Vince, Leo, Scott, Tim, Carey, Christian, and me. As we continue to talk, the distance between us begins to close. It gives way to an openness and candor about the journey just ahead. This is a first-time experience for all of us, although Scott is a marathon runner and Christian has done a fair amount of outdoor activities.

Tim tells us that he and Carey trained by carrying their packs up and down the stairs of their apartment building in New York. They seem fit, ready, and confident, with an appropriate measure of normal anxiety mixed in. One by one, we begin to talk about how each had decided to make the climb and how we trained.

Leo says that he began thinking about the idea of climbing Mount Kilimanjaro after meeting a fellow at a trade show who told him all about it, saying that he (Leo) should go. "It's a great adventure. The mountain is about 9,000 feet high; you don't need to be an experienced climber and you get to see Africa."

The idea stuck. Leo decided he would do it. He announced his intentions to his family and friends and began to make the logistical preparations. It was not until six or eight weeks later that he realized that Kilimanjaro was not 9,000 feet—but over 19,000 feet! But by then, it was too late. He was committed.

Vince asks me about my experience climbing and my training. I admit that I have never done any climbing before. In terms of training, I tell the group that I live on a university campus, just a few doors down from my office; and yet, I still drive to work. So I had to really work at getting enough training. We also talk about the challenge of trying to prepare for the riggers of the high altitude. For this, no one knows what to expect.

Shortly after breakfast, we gather for our first official meeting. We are joined by two Africans who introduce themselves as our guides. The head guide's name is Nickson Moshe. He is 34 and has been climbing for about 15 years. Nickson is tall, handsome, and friendly, yet professional. The assistant guide is a man named Freddie. He is a colorful character with lots of personality and a bright orange and green cap.

For the next two hours, Nickson and Freddie take us step-by-step through the trip. They tell us that our original itinerary to the Western Breach will have to be modified in light of the death of the Americans on that same route two weeks earlier. Once we reach about 14,000 feet, we will change our course and move laterally across the face of the mountain to intersect another route for the push to the summit.

10:40 A.M.

We conclude this briefing and gather our gear. We then check any bags not being taken to the mountain with the staff at the front desk of the lodge. One of the important things I did this morning was to inventory, one last time, my equipment and supplies for the trip. I want to be sure I have not forgotten anything and that nothing has come up missing in the various transfers of my baggage. Knowing that nearly everything I brought will have to be carried up the mountain, I have tried my best to pack only the bare essentials. I am leaving one small bag at the lodge containing a change of clothes for my trip home.

Once everything is in order, we load into two Land Rovers for a trip to a campsite on the western slope. The air is clear, warm, and filled with anticipation as we pull away from the lodge. After nearly an hour, the paved road ends and we continue on a gravel road for another 20 minutes. Then this gravel road becomes a single-track dirt road. We follow the road into thick trees and sometime later come to a place called Ndarakwai Camp.

It is a permanent wilderness camp of just over 10,000 acres

on an isolated slope of Kilimanjaro. The camp is set under the spreading branches of Acacia trees. The place was named long ago by the Maasai for the large number of trees. With views of both Mount Kilimanjaro and Mount Meru, the camp is nestled in a lush forest of towering fig, podo, and yellow-barked acacias that line the seasonal Ngare Nairobi River. The facilities here include eight spacious tents with thatched roofs and a large separate dining area. There is no electricity or running water, so candles and kerosene lamps give the camp a soft glow once the sun sets.

The site is well maintained with a full staff. The camp's resident manager is a woman who seems to be firmly in control. She greets us as we arrive, assigns our accommodations, discusses the times for our meals, and gives orders to the rest of the staff concerning our bags and gear. Interestingly, her name is "Happy." She validated her name with a constant smile and pleasant manner.

1:15 P.M.

After being taken to our tents, we stow our gear and then gather under a large open pavilion for a lunch of stew and rice, chipotles, and fruit. Following lunch, Thomas Kuyu, one of the staff members from the camp, offers to take us on a walking safari of the area.

We all agree that an extended walk will help us shake off the jet lag and begin the process of getting used to the long days of walking that will soon follow. We assemble at the entrance to the camp, cameras ready. Thomas joins us, carrying a large rifle. "You never know," he says, with no expression.

With Thomas in the lead, we walk south out of the camp and are soon completely surrounded by the tall grass and trees of the savanna. Thomas moves with ease as we follow along a moderately worn walking path. Soon we are with the animals.

First, off to our right about a hundred yards away is a small herd of zebra. Shutters begin to click and telescopic lenses reach forward for a better image.

To the other side, I notice a graceful parade of gazelles leaping effortlessly as they pass by. At our feet and on the trees around us are the unmistakable signs of elephants, lots of them. Keeping us company as we walk is a platoon of baboons and a seemingly endless array of exotic birds. The walk is invigorating as we push further from camp.

About 25 minutes into the walk, we come over a small rise; Thomas stops suddenly and motions for us to be still. There in the near distance is a stand of water buffalo, staring at us, pawing the ground and snorting in agitation. No one moves. Thomas steps forward slightly toward the large bull. The animal twitches nervously, never taking his eyes off Thomas. It is a test of wills. After a few moments, when we fail to advance any closer, the animals turn and move away laterally to the right and the large male continues to hold steady, watching to see if we will follow. When we do not, he, too, turns and joins the group.

After a time, someone in our group, walking off to the side calls to Thomas, "Come here." We all turn and move in that direction. It is Tim. He, Carey, and Christian are standing near a small tree. As we draw closer we can see a zebra on the ground before them.

Thomas approaches the animal carefully, rifle in hand. The zebra is alive, but appears to be near the point of death. Thomas tries to help the animal up, however it is too weak to move. "I think he has been bitten by a snake. I am afraid we have no choice but to leave him here to die," Thomas says. Some take a few pictures and we walk slowly away wishing there was something that could have been done.

Within another half hour, we come within sight of a Maasai

village. Thomas explains to us that this enclosure houses a large extended family of two brothers who live here with their wives and children. We walk to the edge of the village where Thomas talks for a moment with the men at the entrance. They reach some agreement, and Thomas tells us we can enter the small village and take pictures.

There is a group of women tending a large number of goats and there are scores of little children. Thomas informs us that one of the brothers has three wives and the other brother has eight.

The Maasai are very friendly but not many speak English. Soon the young men of the village begin to appear herding cattle in from a full day of grazing. The cattle are moved into a large open corral at the center of the village for the night. The cows are milked and inspected.

4:45 P.M.

Since the afternoon light is beginning to dissipate, using a radio of some type, Thomas calls to the camp. Two vehicles soon arrive to drive us back. This has been a fascinating afternoon on foot out on the open plains surrounded by animals, plants, and the indigenous people of Africa. We arrive at camp just before dusk. I freshen up, as best I can with no running water, and walk the narrow path to the center of camp where the group is already beginning to gather for dinner. The conversation is lively as we relive the walk and the visit with the Maasai. These shared experiences begin to form us into a group. A sense of camaraderie is starting to develop.

I walk with the aid of a flashlight to my tent, which is illuminated now with the glow of an oil lamp. I think back across the day; in many ways I still can't believe I am on the verge of climbing the greatest mountain in all of Africa. Just before turning out the light, I take a moment to read from Ps. 63: "On my bed I remember you; I think of you through the watches of the night" (v. 6).

Journal: *Sunday 9:20 P.M.*

Tomorrow we will move, just after dawn, to a ranger station where we will officially register for the climb. I am very excited as I turn down the flame in my oil lamp. The sounds of the forest are comforting. I think of the words of the ancient Hebrew prophet who wrote:

> *You will keep him in perfect peace,*
> *Whose mind is stayed on You,*
> *Because he trusts in You.*
> *Trust in the LORD forever,*
> *For in . . . the LORD is everlasting strength.*
> *—Isa. 26:3-4, NKJV*

I lay back thinking of both the power and the presence of God. I am surrounded by the wonders of creation. As we walked the plains today, I sensed the extent of the world around me. Off in the distance were great vistas of savanna; towering above us to the left was the massive mountain, and stretched over it all was a wide, expansive sky. The entire canvas displayed the majesty of God.

Here in the darkness, I think about how a journey like the one I am on imposes a certain set of disciplines. There is the discipline of letting go—laying aside, at least for the moment, the things that normally fill my day. My sense is that it is good for me to do this, but it is difficult. I am conditioned to be thinking, "What next?"

This letting go is followed by another set of disciplines, which are all associated with the climb. Within the next few hours, I will have to fully embrace the discipline of focusing solely on the daily challenge at my feet. I am sure that I will need to discipline myself to keep taking each next step, no matter how difficult it may seem. My spirit must focus on the discipline of prayer and meditation as

I set aside the media bombardments that often overtake me. There is also the discipline of faith that will have to be in place, so that fear does not become my constant companion.

PRAYER

Heavenly Father, I thank You for reminding me today of Your constant care and for showing me the wonders of this land. I pray for the villagers I saw and spoke with; watch over them. Tomorrow as the climb begins in earnest, help me to let go of everything that robs me of peace or diminishes the awareness of Your presence in my life. As I move through the course of the climb, may I find true spiritual rest and refreshment, knowing that You are with me and are reaching out, even now, so that I might cast all of my care upon You. Amen.

SECTION TWO

THE PRINCIPLE OF PERSEVERANCE

Nothing in the world can take the place of persistence. Talent will not; nothing is more common than unsuccessful men with talent. Genius will not; unrewarded genius is almost a proverb. Education will not; the world is full of educated derelicts. Persistence and determination are omnipotent. The slogan "press on" has solved and always will solve the problems of the human race.
—Calvin Coolidge

6
THE CLIMB BEGINS
FOREST CAMP

There, ahead, all he could see, as wide as all the world,
great, high, and unbelievably white in the sun,
was the square top of Kilimanjaro.
—Ernest Hemingway, *The Snows of Kilimanjaro*

Overnight: Forest Camp (9,500 feet)

Journal: *Monday, January 23*

The climb begins for real today. I am nervous; in fact, it is more than that. The truth is, I am a little fearful. Yesterday's camping and short walk were a good tune-up. It also helped begin the process of forging us together as a group. Knowing that I am not alone in this is helpful; still, the level of my uneasiness remains high.

It is quite an unusual experience for me to be so out of my comfort zone. Normally, I live a controlled, well-managed life. It is the only way I can keep up with the demands of my work. Being a college president is often very difficult; and yet you get accustomed to the stress and strain. Someone once said the only way to survive in such a job is to start out running as fast as you can and then, over time, pick up the pace! So I am used to meeting the challenges of a rigorous daily routine, but this is different. It calls for an entirely different set of skills and attitudes.

At breakfast, I take a tablet for malaria, which I had begun taking two weeks ago at home. Then I swallow the first Diamox tablet. This is the medicine I have brought along to help prevent altitude sickness. I had been a little uneasy about taking it because of the possible side effects, which I'd read about some months ago

while scanning various online journals from other climbers.
Nevertheless, I want to give myself every chance of making it to the
top, and altitude sickness is the single biggest hurdle to overcome.

After a hearty breakfast we gather at the entrance to the camp to load our things into the Land Rovers for the final transfer to Londorossi Pass (5,900 feet) where we will begin the climb. There are six possible routes to the summit:

The Marangu Route is the oldest and most popular trail and the one that comes closest to the original route used by Hans Meyer in making the first successful assault on the summit. It is the only trail where there are huts that can be used for overnight shelter.

The Machame Route is the second most popular trail and the one that many guides consider the most enjoyable. Though generally considered more difficult than the Marangu Route, the success rate on this trail is higher, perhaps because it is a day longer, which gives climbers an added day for acclimatization.

The Rongai Route is the only trail to approach Kibo from the north. In fact, the original trail began right against the Kenyan border, though in more recent years the trail shifted eastward and now starts near the Tanzanian town of Loitokitok. The trail is now occasionally referred to as the Loitokitok Route.

The Umbwe Route is considered by many to be the most difficult trail. It amounts to a tough vertical climb through the jungle where one uses the tree roots as makeshift rungs on a ladder.

The Shira Route and the Lemosho trails run from west to east across the heart of the high Shira Plateau. These two routes are perhaps the least popular trails on the mountain. The Shira Route is the original plateau trail though seldom used these days, having given way to the Lemosho Route.

The Lemosho Route is a fairly new trail that improves on the Shira Route by starting below the Shira Ridge, thus providing trekkers with both a walk in the forest at the start of the trek and more time to acclimatize during the long walk across the Shira Plateau. On this route, the summit is reached by scaling the western break of the crater wall and then up to Uhuru Peak.

I have chosen the Lemosho, Western Breach, route for my climb. This is a long and demanding way to go with a final campsite at 18,750 feet inside Kilimanjaro's dormant volcanic crater. However, it offers the best chance of success because it allows for more time to adjust to the high altitude. The trail head is at a place called Lemosho Glades, where the road comes to an end in a high forest clearing. We must first stop to register at an entrance to the National Park at the edge of a mountain village named Londorossi.

Once we have loaded our gear into and onto the vehicles, we say farewell to the staff of the camp. A porter, a nice young man standing near the vehicles, waves as we slowly begin to pull away. He smiles and says, *"Upande mlima kwa usalama na mafanikio"* (Have a safe and successful climb).

"Asante."

Although there are several Maasai villages in the area, such as the one we visited yesterday, most of the people of the western slope are the Chagga people. They are less nomadic than the Maasai. The Chagga established permanent towns and have developed agriculture as a basis for their way of life.

As with the rest of tropical Africa, it was through missionary schools that western forms of education came to the ordinary people of Kilimanjaro. Missionary Johann Rebmann, the first European to visit the mountain (see chapter 1), arrived in 1848 in the company of Swahili Arab merchants who introduced him to the Chagga chieftains of Kilema and Machame. But it was not until 1886 that the first permanent missionaries were sent to establish a mission station at Machame and then Moshi. However, this English initiative was short-lived because of the recasting of the border separating Kenya (which was English) and Tanzania (which was German).

English missionaries were soon replaced by work carried on by the German Lutheran Missionary Society of Leipzig, Germany. Later, in the mid-1890s, French Catholic missionaries from the order of Spiritans or Holy Ghost Fathers pushed inland from their long-established settlements near Bagamoyo. Once arriving in the region of Kilimanjaro, the Spiritans established mission stations at Kilema, Kibosho, and Rombo.

We pass through many small towns and villages as we make our way slowly up and around the lower slopes toward our destination. The last few miles are heavily wooded and fairly steep. Although the road is paved, it is particularly narrow and in poor repair.

While driving up to our final staging and departure area, we catch several breathtaking views of the top of Kilimanjaro. I cannot imagine walking my way to the sky and standing up there; yet that is exactly what I hope to do. As we make a series of twists and turns moving back and forth up the mountain, the peak appears, disappears, and suddenly reappears in what seems to be a different position at every sighting. It is as if the mountain is alive and moving.

There are also times when we think we are seeing the top, only to realize it is not the peak at all. As we are talking about this, Christian points out that there will be times during the climb when we will see "false peaks," while the real mountain peak remains hidden somewhere beyond the visible horizon.

How like life.

We finally arrive in the town of Londorossi. It is a bustling place and appears to be prosperous by regional standards. At the far edge of the town there is a government station where we must present our passports and sign the register for the climb. One by one we stand at a window and reach in to sign our names in a large book.

Then we wait. The porters will meet us here with all of the supplies. Soon they arrive and begin repacking the supplies into bundles and bags that can be carried on foot once we begin the trek. This procedure takes well over an hour. While we wait, a group of the porters sets up a large lunch table and begins to lay out fruit and sandwiches. We gather to eat.

As we are eating, we hear voices, many voices, excited voices coming from the trees at the edge of our clearing. As our eyes adjust to the shadows of the forest, we can see children, 10 or 15 of them, peering through the trees. Tim calls to them—no response. One of the porters tells us that there is a school nearby on the other side of the small government compound. The children are from that school.

After a few minutes, Tim takes a large tray of oranges, bananas, and sliced papaya and walks to the edge of the trees. Finally one brave young boy steps forward out of the shadows; a stampede follows—the children squeal and laugh as they grab for the fruit.

Following the meal, a signal is given and we gather at the vans for a few final instructions. We will load and drive the short distance to where the road is no more. There everything will be unloaded and so will we. It is now about 12:30 P.M.

Everyone seems unusually quiet during the short drive. The road ends abruptly in a wide opening among the trees. Everybody out. Backpacks are checked one last time, gaiters are strapped on, poles are adjusted, and pictures are taken. Reality is now staring us in the face. In just a few moments we will be underway. The challenge of the climb itself now takes on an

added dimension as the group gets organized to strike out for the first day of climbing.

Soon I will find out if the real mountain will match the mountain of my imagination. I think it already does!

Unceremonially, Nickson calls for us to depart. Joachim, a third guide who has joined us with the supplies, leads the way as Nickson and Freddie remain with the porters for the last bit of organization and packing. They will catch up to us in the forest. We turn from what little is left of civilization, our vehicles with their radios, and walk single file into a narrow opening in the bush—we're off.

I am surprised, almost immediately, at how cool it is under the tall trees and hanging vines. We quickly settle into a rhythm as we learn to coordinate the movement of our feet with the poles. The weight of my pack begins to make its presence known. I become aware that my center of gravity is different because of the nearly 20 pounds on my back. It doesn't seem too bad until the trail starts upward. I am a bit shocked at how steep it is, and I am amused to think that this surprises me. How could I have not anticipated such a steep incline? It is a mountain after all!

I feel the pack pull me backward as I move up the mountain and begin to adjust my movements in harmony with its presence. At several places, we have to climb our way slowly up steep embankments and over large outcroppings. We move farther and farther through the dense rain forest (which receives approximately 80 inches of precipitation per year) and under the tangled canopy of moss-coated vines, which is home to the black and white colobus monkey, blue monkey, and a vibrant array of exotic birds.

An hour or so into the walk, we hear voices coming up behind us; it is the porters hauling the supplies. One by one they move quickly past us. *"Jambo!"* Each young man is carrying on his shoulders a large bundle. It is embarrassing to see them, with such heavy loads, passing us with apparent ease. We immediately begin to appreciate the vital role these workers will play in the success of our climb.

Once they are past, we settle back into a steady pace, twisting and turning our way along. Within a few minutes, we come to a large tree that has fallen across the way. We cannot go around it, nor can we move it. So we do what climbers do, we crawl up and over the large trunk stretched out before us. Joachim goes first, step by step—a hand pull here and there and he is over. He makes it look easy; particularly because in addition to his backpack, he is carrying a bundle of about six dozen eggs tied together with string and soft corrugated cardboard. "I guess it will be scrambled eggs for breakfast," Leo says, as he notices the eggs.

One by one we try to replicate Joachim's traverse. As I begin to step up and over the first few sections of the fallen tree, I realize just how stiff and unagile I am. The younger climbers seem to move with ease. "I am coming," I call out, as most of the group waits on the other side. Relieved, I finally straddle the last section and plant both feet firmly back on the trail. This will prove to be only the first of many such obstacles. When the last member joins the group, we turn and begin again.

I don't know how it happened, but just as we start to climb up away from the tree, I trip and fall. In a flash I am down on the ground. It is humbling to be the first to fall, particularly since we are now standing on relatively flat ground. Vince and Scott help me up. "I'm sorry," I said.

"No problem," Christian calls out. "It could happen to any of us."

Just then, our guide Joachim yells in a loud voice, "Ants!" Immediately, he drops to his knees at my feet and begins picking something off of my shoes. African ants—they are everywhere. We begin to stomp and scramble and scurry up the trail. In a few moments, we stop to inspect our boots.

"Ouch!" Christian shouts. There is at least one ant or maybe more in his pants leg. He slaps and swats and dances like he's at a discotheque. We watch helplessly as he battles these tiny warriors. After a few moments, he stops. Evidently he has killed the ant(s) but not before being bitten. And Carey, too, is squirming. There is an ant in her shirt. She is also bitten. They both say that it feels like a terrible bee sting. We rest for a while to allow them a few minutes to adjust to the pain and recover from their brief trauma. No one ever mentioned it, but I somehow feel that this episode is my fault, that my fall had stirred a nest of ants and sent them on the war path.

We continue to climb for nearly two more hours. Fatigued, we eventually arrive at the base of a large, steep hill covered with vegetation. From the top of the hill we hear voices. We must be close to camp. That thought renews our determination.

I garner my energy and begin to climb my way up to the top. Every step is taxing. I keep stretching, pulling, and climbing my way upward. As I finally make it to the top of the hill, I can see in front of me a large flat clearing in the trees; it is Forest Camp. What a relief.

The first thing I do as I enter the camp is to slip the pack from my back and unbuckle my gaiters. My shoulders are aching. I see my gray bag sitting outside one of the small sleeping tents. Freddie is there, helping us get organized.

"This will be your tent, John."

"Thank you, Freddie."

I pull off my shoes and crawl in for a brief inspection. This will be the first time I have slept in a tent since I was in the fourth grade. My friend Steve and I slept out in my backyard, and I thought we were really roughing it then. All we had was a radio, a plate of homemade cookies, lots of blankets, and a porch-lit path to an indoor restroom 35 feet in front of the tent. That wasn't camping, it was recreation.

My tent tonight is surrounded by dense forest, miles from the nearest road, and half a globe from home with no running water, no restroom, no plate of homemade cookies, and no electricity. I want my mommy!

I unroll a pad and place it on the floor of the tent and then pull my sleeping bag from the duffle. It stretches the length of the tent. I give it a shake to let it breathe a bit. Then Ronald, one of the porters, calls to me from outside.

"Tea is ready," he says in a soft voice.

"Thanks, Ronald."

He has brought a small plastic basin of water to the front of my tent.

I wash my hands and splash some water on my face, turn to zip my tent flap shut, and walk with Leo to a large green tent.

We poke our heads in to see the rest of our group already sitting inside around a table. There are biscuits, sliced papaya, and hot tea. We take our places. It's not home, but it's not bad.

I ask Christian about the ant bites. He tells us he can still feel them, but the pain is pretty well gone. Tim then turns the conversation to the color of Leo's duffle bag. It is bright pink. "What's with the pink bag, Leo? Anything we should know?"

Vince picks up the conversation, "I've been wondering about that since we met at the airport. It's a little 'girly,' isn't it?"

Leo, not even looking up, replies, "It takes a real man to climb Kili with a pink bag; besides, it was on sale!"

Following tea, we return to the tents to get our gear stowed away. I slip off my walking boots and crawl back into the tent. I need to figure out how to navigate inside such a small area. I shift the sleeping bag a little right of center, just enough to get the duffle bag pulled up beside me. I start to unload what I will need for the night. I take out my flashlight and my headlamp. I want to make sure I can find them once the sun goes down.

After arriving at the campsite, the porters had walked to a nearby stream to fill a large drum with water. Once we get our tents organized, we gather around the water with our handheld pumps and empty water bottles. However, rather than having to fill the bottles ourselves, one of the porters has been assigned this task. He tells us, in broken English, to leave the bottles. He will fill them during supper. In watching him, I can see that he seems pleased to have a responsible job. He is careful to keep the bottles separate. One by one he pumps the water through a small, handheld filter into each bottle. Later, after retrieving our individual bottles, each of us will treat the water with chemical tablets to kill the bacteria.

As the light fades, the shadows become particularly large and animated. The silhouette of the peak is barely visible through the trees. The mountain is a solid thing with a life of its own. Its shadow prowls along the heights and valleys around me. Coolness fills the air.

Evening arrives quickly; as darkness ends this first day on the mountain, I am pleased and satisfied to be well on the way. I am tired and yet my spirit resists those realities, for this day and this moment will not last long, and I don't want to miss it. The fatigue and hunger will pass. I hope to hold the memories of this day and this sunset moment with me for a long time. Just after dark, our evening meal is served. First there is hot soup, followed by pasta with a meat sauce, fresh fruit, coffee or tea. It is fairly good, given the circumstances and the fact that we are all pretty hungry.

Just as we finish eating, Nickson and Freddie join us. "How is everyone? Anyone having trouble?" Tim says he thinks he is already starting to develop blisters; everyone else is fine. "We will wake you at 6:30, breakfast will be at about 7:15, and we will start off from camp at 8:00. Tomorrow we will climb out of the trees into the heath zone. We will have lunch around noon and then make our way to Shira Camp," Nickson tells us.

After leaving the meal, I walk back toward the tents. Leo, Vince, Scott, and I stand to talk for a few minutes and then, one by one, we walk to our separate tents. Although I am with my new friends, I am feeling alone tonight. Home seems such a long way away.

Before I crawl in for the night, I look up. It is as if I have never seen stars before. This sight of the African sky is truly stunning. The air is thin; there is no pollution or ambient light to mar the view. I am transfixed. As I stand here, on the slopes of Kilimanjaro, I hear only the wind in the trees. I think back over the day. I look up once more. As I see the stars, I recall the words of the psalmist, which I committed to memory during my days of training for the climb. The words come alive in night air.

O LORD, our Lord,
how majestic is your name in all the earth!
You have set your glory above the heavens.
From the lips of children and infants
you have ordained praise
because of your enemies,
to silence the foe and the avenger.
When I consider your heavens,
the work of your fingers,
the moon and the stars,
which you have set in place,
what is man that you are mindful of him,
the son of man that you care for him?
You made him a little lower than the heavenly beings
and crowned him with glory and honor.
You made him ruler over the works of your hands;
you put everything under his feet:
all flocks and herds,
and the beasts of the field,
the birds of the air,
and the fish of the sea,
all that swim the paths of the seas.
O LORD, our Lord,
how majestic is your name in all the earth!

—Ps. 8

This view of the night sky already makes the trip worth the toil and effort. As I continue to scan the heavens, I remember that I should be able to see the Southern Cross. The Southern Cross is perhaps the best known and most recognizable star group in the southern hemisphere. This constellation's distinctive shape is easily located because of its brightness and the proximity of each star to the others.

The Southern Cross contains a set of bright stars situated so that they depict the extremities of a Latin cross. Thousands of years ago these stars were an object of reverence in the Near East. In biblical days, they were visible just above the horizon. However, this cluster of stars was last seen from the latitude of Jerusalem at the time of the crucifixion of Christ; since then it can only be seen from the southern hemisphere.

European sailors rediscovered the constellation in the early 16th century; they used it for direction and to calculate the time of day. Because it is not visible in the northern skies, there are no Greek or Roman myths or legends associated with it. It does appear, however, in the poetry of Europe, once the sailors from those nations began to traverse the southern seas.

To the Southern Cross

by James Stanley Gilbert

When evening drapes her filmy robe
*   O'er distant hill and drooping palm,*
And, save soft echoes, naught disturbs
*   The purple twilight's drowsy calm—*

Soft echoes from the coral reef;
*   The waves' low greeting to the stars,*
That, answering across the sea,
*   Send fellowship on shining bars—*

'Tis then, while earth is slumbering,
*   Its woes forgot in restful dreams,*
That thou, Christ's love-test symbolling,
*   Shed'st o'er the blue thy sacred beams.*

'Tis then by him who, listening, waits,
*   The still, small voice is heard again*

In song—the sweetest ever sung—
"Upon earth peace: good-will to men!"[7]

Once I am in for the night, I realize there is a large flap covering the inside top of the tent. I had not noticed it earlier. As I unzip the flap it reveals the presence of a wide clear plastic pane—a skylight! This is terrific. I can lie here in the sleeping bag and look up at the stars; in fact, I can see the cross and sleep under its soft glow. God is good.

It is a fascinating experience to be here. In a way it seems dangerous and it is; yet, this is a peaceful place. Is there a better place to lie still than among a great stand of trees? The forest surrounds me, and He who made the forest watches over me as I rest in stillness, quiet, and reverie.

I am alone; nonetheless, I am not alone, for God is here. With my eyes closed I lie still and listen to the silence. After a few minutes, I begin to realize that, in a way, the only true time a person can properly call his or her own is that which he or she has all to himself or herself; the rest belongs to others. So I thank God for this moment alone, under the African sky. I offer a final prayer for the day, asking God to help me draw strength from this solitude. Perhaps by being alone, my presence back in society will be more authentic.

PRAYER

Dear God, maker of heaven and earth, thank You for watching over us today. I sensed Your presence in the forest and Your help during the difficult parts of the climb. I know You are with me. I feel Your presence. As I look through the top of this small tent, I see Your wide heavens. I think of the words of the psalmist, "For great is your love, higher than the heavens; your faithfulness reaches to the skies. Be exalted, O God, above the heavens, and let your glory be over all the earth" (Ps. 108:4-5). This is my prayer. Amen.

7
A HAUNTING REVERENCE
SHIRA ONE CAMP

Keep your face to the sunshine and you cannot see the shadow.
—Helen Keller

Overnight: Shira One Camp (12,200 feet)

Journal: *Tuesday, January 24*

"Hello, John!" a voice calls from outside my tent. As I awake, it is already light.

"*Jambo,*" I reply. "Is that Ronald?"

"Yes, I have brought you water and coffee."

I slide out of my sleeping bag and reach down to unzip the flap of the tent. Ronald's smile greets me.

"Good morning, Ronald."

"Did you sleep well?" he asks.

"Yes."

"Breakfast will be in about 20 minutes."

"Thank you."

I pull my coffee back into the tent with me and look out at the trees standing guard around us. The light coming through the forest canopy dapples our campsite in dancing shade and shadow. It seems a bit cool outside, but the air is fresh and clean.

As I sip myself awake, I suddenly realize how stiff I am. I lie back and lift my knees, one at a time to my chin. This hurts and feels good at the same time. My shoulders are tender from the weight of the backpack. I pull on a fresh shirt and exchange my fleece pants for climbing clothes.

I scoot myself out of the tent and I slip on my boots. I stand for a moment taking in the morning. The sun is already bright, though diffused by the leaves. The porters are singing an odd mixture of tribal songs and Lutheran hymns, evidently passed down to them by German missionaries.

I find a place to stand and wash with the little bit of water Ronald left for me at the opening of my tent. I want to do my best to stay as clean as possible, which I can already tell will not be easy. The water on my face feels good. I brush my teeth and return to my tent, just as the call for breakfast is sounded. Hot cereal, bananas, sliced oranges, and toast are on the table. Coffee and tea are available. Soon, one of the porters enters with a large platter of scrambled eggs. I look at Leo and smile. "Joachim," he says. I nod. As I finish the meal, I take a second Diamox tablet. So far, so good.

Everyone is energetic as we finish the meal and head back to our tents to pack up our gear. I check my backpack carefully. Everything is in order. I store my sleeping bag and other items

in the gray duffle and set it outside the tent. I strap on my gaiters and check my poles.

There is a genuine sense of anticipation as we get ready for the first full day of climbing. Yesterday was just a teaser. Today, we get down (or should I say up) to business. We gather at the edge of the camp for our final briefing from Nickson; then off we go, single file, back into the forest.

The path we are on ascends smoothly and gently as the forest begins to thin and the vegetation surrounding the trail alters. Over time, the taller trees give way and the thick underbrush diminishes. After about three and a half hours, we emerge out of the heavy forest into the heath zone with its giant heathers. Now that we are at the upper reaches of the tree line, the vistas expand exponentially. We can see for miles in nearly every direction.

The gradient increases as the path progresses, leveling only now and then to cross one of the many small streams here. From this point there are sweeping views of the entire rolling, crumpled plateau as it stretches southeast. Still out in front of us, to the right, is the Shira Ridge and on it are the highest points of the Shira Plateau, Johnsell Point, and Klute Peak.

After climbing for another hour and a half, we stop in one of the last shaded areas to rest for a few moments and have lunch. The porters have erected a tent. It feels good to drop the pack and sit for a time in a chair. As the food is brought in, I don't seem to be hungry. I take a few slices of orange and some bread and cheese, but nothing tastes good. I drink as much water as I can while we rest, and pull out a small packet of cookies from my pack. At least these will give me some energy, I tell myself.

Soon we are back on the go. The pack is riding more easily on my shoulders today. I am so thankful to be getting used to that weight. Yesterday, it was very annoying. Now, I am still aware of the pack, but it is not as bad.

Tim, from New York, is the one having trouble. The blisters he was beginning to notice late yesterday are starting to trouble him again. At a brief rest stop for water, he pulls his boots off to inspect the damage. His feet are getting worse, and it is just the second day. I wonder how long he can last. Before rebooting, he adds a few Band-Aids and a second pair of socks.

The trail is not too difficult. There are stretches when we have to tackle a strenuous climb, but these are followed by a gentle slope back downward. Our task is to reach the top of the ridge that marks the western edge of the great Shira Plateau. We will have to work hard from this point on to make it to the top.

The top of the ridge is now just before us. As the climb intensifies, I begin to wonder if I can hold out through all of this. This is very tough going. I am fearful that this will seem like nothing, once we hit the higher altitudes. It is just the second day, and I am already beginning to wish this experience was over. I stop for a minute to push those ideas out of my mind.

"Don't go there," I tell myself. "Just keep walking and climb when you have to climb; it will be all right."

Finally, by midafternoon, we reach the high point of the ridge. The path crests the western edge of the Shira Plateau at about 12,500 feet. We stop for water and a few minutes of rest. Nickson points into the distance where we can just barely see the porters. "We will camp tonight out there on the plateau," he tells us.

As we begin again, the path drops slightly as it negotiates heathers and small boulder outcroppings on its way down to the Shira One Camp. The view we now have of the upper regions of Kilimanjaro from across this plateau is amazing. The mountain wears a beard of cloud and a bonnet of snow.

Once the trail stretches out beyond the back side of the ridge, the climb takes a steep track downward into a savanna of tall grasses, heather, and volcanic rock draped with lichen beards. This is followed by an ascent through the lush rolling hills that gives way to the broad plain of the Shira Plateau.

Finally, after nearly seven hours of trekking, we reach the next campsite still at the western edge of the plateau. Once again, I am so glad to drop my pack and pull off my boots. We leave our nearly empty water bottles in the center of camp as our new friend, the porter, begins once more to refill them while we rest. After about a half hour stretched out in my tent, I hear voices outside. I wrestle my way out of the tent and find a place to sit with Vince, Leo, Scott, and Freddie.

What does it take to establish a relationship with a group of strangers with whom you will share the experience of a lifetime? These fellow climbers will see me at my best and worst and then perhaps never see me again. I have already noticed a few things that seem to characterize the relationship within my new band of brothers (and one sister). Almost immediately there was a genuine spirit of acceptance. Everyone is taken at face value. No judgments about one another seem to be made too soon. If one of us needs a little more time getting ready or stops to take a photo and lingers a little too long, the groups displays patience and care.

There is also a tone of encouragement that marks our conversation. In short, without ever talking about it or taking a vote, we have set the golden rule as our standard. We all know we need each other. Even now, with the trip still in its early stages, we sense that we are in this together for good or ill.

There is also a good measure of laughter among the group, beginning with the comments about Leo's pink duffle bag. Victor Borge was correct when he observed, "Laughter is the shortest distance between two people." The writer Sidney Shelton made a curious comment when he wrote, "Do not judge strangers harshly. Remember that every stranger you meet is you."[8] We were strangers at the bottom of the mountain; we have already become friends and my sense is that we may well be family at the summit.

As we sit and talk, I begin to sense that there is a haunting reverence in this place. The wind is warm; the sky is pewter. The top of Kilimanjaro still looms out before us. The band of clouds covering its face has begun to slowly give way.

I stand and then walk away from the others to look at the mountain as it is transformed before me. I watch in silence for some time. The mist finally clears and then, suddenly, the last rays of sunlight are refracted by the high mountain air into tongues of fire creating a Pentecost of light at sunset. What majesty. It was the German philosopher, Goethe, who said, "Nature is the living visible garment of God." Time floats for a moment as I stand transfixed by this display.

"Do any human beings ever realize life while they live it?—every, every minute?" asks Emily in *Our Town*. At this point in Thornton Wilder's play, Emily is a ghost; she has just died and is allowed a brief visit back to life. To her question, the stage manager gives this answer, "No." Then after a pause adds, "The saints and poets, maybe—they do some."

Collette, the French novelist who died at 81, had a full and meaningful life, but at one point she wrote, "What a wonderful life I've had! I only wish I'd realized it sooner." Her words are bittersweet. How important it is to have a sense of the now and the wonder of simply being alive.

Soon, too soon, the light show is over. I turn to see Vince standing nearby. "Wow, that was really something," he said.

"Vince, there are only a handful of people in the entire world who will ever see what we have just witnessed." We walk away in silence.

Before long we are all gathered in the tent for the evening meal. Soup, potatoes, chicken (I think?) and rice, vegetables, bread, fruit, and cookies. I am not hungry, but I take a little soup to start. It actually tastes pretty good, although it looks like dirty dishwater. I try some rice and vegetables but leave more on my plate than I am able to eat. It must be the altitude or the exertion that is suppressing my appetite. I am sure I will feel better tomorrow.

Nickson and Freddie join us at the end of the meal. Tomorrow will be a lighter day, set aside to help us adjust to the altitude. We will leave around 8:30 to make our way slowly across the wide expanse of the plateau. We will travel several miles but will be gaining only about 1,000 feet in altitude before we make camp at Shira Two.

After the meal, I walk slowly back to the tent. I am really tired and yet it feels good to be making progress, and I am encouraged that tomorrow will be an easier day. I stop at my tent to look up again. Because we are now clearly up beyond the trees, the sky is even more majestic than last night at Forest Camp.

There is such depth and texture to the heavens. I fix my eyes again upon the Southern Cross. How reassuring to realize that I will sleep tonight and each night of this journey under the cross. I am comforted to know that even in this faraway place, the love of God overshadows my lying down and my rising up.

I unzip the tent and inch my way back into my canvas condo. I slip out of the clothes I wore and into a fleece sweat suit for sleeping. My muscles are weary, but I don't seem particularly sore. My feet are fine, no sign of blisters.

Before crawling into my sleeping bag, I go back through my gear. To my surprise, I come upon a card, tucked under my things at the far end of my duffle bag. How is it possible that I did not find this before at the lodge when I inspected my things after the flight or on either of the last two nights?

I pull the card out into the light of my head lamp. It is from Jill. Written on the envelope is this message, "John, open evening of January 21 or later." I lift the card from the envelope and read the words printed on the front and inside. I can hardly believe my eyes; it was as if it were perfectly planned, for before me is a marvelous poem about a star twinkling messages of love to me. How had Jill known? Suddenly it was as if she were there with me under the starry sky. At the bottom of the card she had written, "I'll be thinking of you every day."

PRAYER

God of heaven and earth, I thank You for Your faithfulness and care. You are here, even here in this remote place. How glad I am to have the assurance that You do not simply watch my life from a distance. You are not a spectator, sitting in the stands. You are active in the unfolding moments of days and nights. I do not know what tomorrow will bring. I leave it in Your hands. Give me rest and peace for tonight and be with Jill. Amen.

8
ONE STEP AT A TIME
SHIRA TWO CAMP

Open all your pores and bathe in all the tides of nature.
—Henry David Thoreau

Overnight: Shira Two Camp (12,600 feet)

Journal: *Wednesday, January 25*

I awake to wonder . . . what a morning. It is just dawn. I want to get up and not get up, at the same time.

After a few moments, I summon the willpower to crawl out of my sleeping bag and pull open the flap of the tent. I am calmed and energized by the sight of the high mountain plateau waking with me. As the sun rises behind the mass of Kibo and slowly climbs above the peak, it suddenly shifts and shoots brilliant beams of light from the snowcapped heights of the mountain. These morning fireworks of light are invigorating.

There are many wonders to be experienced on Kilimanjaro. From the lush equatorial forests bordering the edge of Wachagga fields of maize and beans, through the ethereal upper moorland with its bizarre plants, to the upper flanks of Kibo with its volcano cathedrals and cliffs of azure-streaked ice; every step of the journey is filled with awe.

As the sun continues to rise, its light slowly begins to tiptoe across the landscape—stepping ever so gently on the small flowers and grasses. Warmth is already starting to caress the rocks. Minute by minute the light changes as it makes its way across the Shira Plateau and the mountain face. In the early moments of the

day it seems that everything sparkles with freshness almost as if this is the first time the sun has ever risen. The tall grass catches the light as it beams its way across the slopes; the rocks glow with color as the mountain takes on a fresh clarity.

We gather for breakfast once more. The same menu! I am sensing a pattern here. I have a small cup of hot cereal with sugar added. I feel a bit nauseous at the sight of this food. The eggs arrive. I take a small spoonful and try to force it down. The orange slices are refreshing, but nothing else seems to satisfy. I was hoping I might have an appetite today. Perhaps I will feel like eating a little later when we stop for lunch.

My companions are all well. Vince and Scott have hearty appetites. Tim and Carey are the last to arrive for breakfast. They are friendly but quiet. I think Tim is worried. Christian is chatty. No one seems to mind, but no one answers him either. He is a pleasant person with a sense of innocence about him.

After breakfast, we return to our tents to gather our things. It is a glorious morning, crisp and sunny. The porters are singing as *they prepare to break camp. Everyone seems to be in a good mood. I am standing just now at the perimeter of our campsite, on a broad flat plain looking back—then looking ahead. Few climbers come this way, so there is a tangible sense of isolation and remoteness here on the edge of the plateau. Shira is one of the highest plateaus on earth, averaging 12,500 feet. It is a land of harsh realities and yet—there is grandeur here.*

Today we are to hike east across the Shira Plateau and camp tonight at Shira Two, at the far edge of the region. This is scheduled to be a lighter day, climbing half the distance vertically that we did yesterday; so that we might more easily adjust to the thinning air.

Nickson calls for us to move out, "Twendai!" I will write more later ...

I walk in silence, listening only to the wind and to my labored breathing. Movement is hard; my steps are more difficult than I thought they might be. Isn't this supposed to be an easier day? I hold steady, take some deep breaths, and keep walking. The light of the morning has intensified enormously. Sweat drips into my eyes. I am surprised at the temperature at this high altitude.

Even though the trekking is more difficult than I anticipated, it is nearly impossible to keep from feeling high-spirited in these hours before the mists arrive to transform the world into a mysterious place. The hills rise and fall, rise and fall, then rise and fall again. I hate it when the terrain pitches us downward. I know that for every step down, we must take another step up at some point. I am surprised at the rolling nature of what appeared to be a flat plain.

The climb is turning out to be longer as well as more demanding than I thought it would be. I made the mistake of believing our guides when they said, "Tomorrow will be a lighter day." I guess it is easier in some ways, but it is not easy. The heat begins to build throughout the day as we talk toward the sun. When we stop for lunch, I put on a light layer of sunscreen. My nose and the back of my neck are beginning to burn. My feet are still good, and my legs seem strong. The pack is now almost undetectable. I hardly know it is on my back.

I talk to myself as we start out again after lunch. I tell myself to walk this land with wonder. Don't be so concerned with getting there that you miss the texture of the journey itself. Sights, sounds, smells, the feel of the soil and the rocks, all create a tapestry that I will not experience again. I must savor this; there is a rhythm and motion of the climb.

By midafternoon the clouds begin to gather and the sight of Kibo is lost. There seems to be an endless rhythm to the coming of the fog each morning and its disappearance each afternoon. The mist drops like a scrim. Our eyes are those of a cataract patient, straining to see beyond odd shapes and figures. Nonetheless, we just keep walking, step after step after step.

When the miasma rolls in, it changes one's interior landscape as well as the world at large. For a few hours each day it is as though Kili is hiding its face. In these moments I hold steady and trust the guide and keep going forward. The mist obscures the view of where we are headed and clouds the trail bearing witness to where we have been.

The path undulates across the surface of the plateau, hugging the lay of the land and following its every detail as it drops into small gullies containing tributary streams of the Ngare Nairobi River and then climbs back up again. All the while the path gradually gains height, passing through an attractive high alpine meadow of heather. To the right of the path are several prominent features that mark this route across the plateau. The Shira

Needle, Shira Cathedral, and East Shira Hills are all jagged points on the ragged ridge that runs along the lip of the plateau.

After a time, the light returns. "The stronger light and the blue sky teach you to see," wrote Van Gogh from Arles, in southern France. He was possessed by an infatuation with the shades of color born by the light of Provence. "The emotions that come over me in the face of nature can be so intense that I nearly lose consciousness," he wrote in his last year.[9]

At a stop for water, Nickson points to a high ridge out in front, just beyond a narrow creek. "Up there, at the top of the ridge is Shira Two. It will take us about 45 more minutes, and then we can rest," he tells us.

Off we go for the final push to camp. It is becoming more difficult to breathe as we climb. I stop two or three times on the ascent of the ridge to catch my breath. Soon we are there, and I sit for a time on a large rock at the top. Even though I am washed out, I realize that this was a good day. We have covered several miles. From this campsite, the summit of Kilimanjaro seems close. Finally we are getting near our destination. The afternoon cloud-cover runs for cover, and the majestic mountain peak stands clearly before us. The sight rivets me—anchors my attention.

I walk to a spot near the center of our camp, where there are a few large rocks and sit for a while sipping the remaining water from the bottles in my backpack. Here, just before me, is my first clear, up close look at the top of the mountain. As I gaze at the summit . . .

I am in awe.

It is awesome.

I'm awestruck.

It is an awe-full moment.

To be awed is to be awakened, to be aware. Awe is an expression of wonder, reverence, and respect, which suggests the presence of something majestic. When we are in the embrace of awe—we are stilled, silent, attentive, and obedient. "Life is not lost by dying; life is lost minute-by-minute, day by dragging day, in all the small uncaring ways."[10]

The mountain slowly reveals itself in ways one cannot see from far away. The soil, the plants, and the air all introduce themselves little by little as one climbs. "Every now and again take a good look at something not made with hands—a mountain, a star, the turn of a stream. There will come to you wisdom and patience and solace and, above all, the assurance that you are not alone in the world."[11]

7:48 P.M.

Following dinner, I walk once more back to my tent. Today is my father's birthday, the first one since his death last October. I delivered a eulogy at his funeral service using the title "Like Father, like Son." A few months before his death, Jill was looking at a photograph in which I was standing with a few other individuals from the university. "You stand just like your dad," she said. Her words set me to thinking. My father was the kind of person who took a stand. He was a man of integrity. He was also kind and generous. I think about him today and hope that I might, in fact, stand just like my dad.

My father would have thought this trip to Kilimanjaro was simply crazy, and yet he would have liked the idea of my pushing the envelope a bit, trying something new. He lived his life and built his business by daily taking the next hill, moving on to accomplish something more.

PRAYER

Heavenly Father, as I lie here for these few moments before

a night of sleep, I am thinking of Your blessings. I am thankful for my heritage and for the example of a good and godly father. May the characteristics of my dad be seen in me as well. And, Lord, how good it is to recall that You come to us as a Father to His children. May I also be worthy to be called a child of God. Amen.

9
DETOUR
BARRANCO CAMP

So why do we bother (to climb)?
Just this: what is above knows what is below,
but what is below does not know what is above.
—René Daumal, philosopher and climber

Overnight: Barranco Camp (12,700 feet)

Journal: *Thursday, January 26*

We make a detour beginning today. Our plan was to continue from the Shira Plateau route to the Machame Route to a campsite at Lava Tower. However, because of the accident two weeks ago, we are forced to make a major adjustment. From Shira Two Camp we move south along the summit circuit as we head toward a place called Barranco Camp. Because we are moving laterally, there is a fair amount of up and down trekking. This breaks the rhythm of the climb.

The trek will cover about 10 miles but will result in a gain of only about 500 feet in altitude. However, this is an important leg of the journey, following the detour. The day will begin to position us for our final ascent several miles to the east and because the walk is relatively light, it will continue to help us with the process of adjusting to the altitude.

Following breakfast, the day begins with a steady, gentle ascent toward our original route of tackling the western slopes of Kibo. Continuing to move through the dry, boulder-strewn terrain of the last stretches of the Shira Plateau, the pathway mean-

ders as it rises and falls, negotiating the gentle folds of the plateau. After an hour or so, this gives way to a shallow incline as we turn fully eastward.

Here the trail is uneven with several difficult descents and alternating scrambles. After a time, the path loops southeast and divides at that point into two. It is at this point that we would have normally headed up toward Lava Tower and a campsite there. However, that route has been abandoned by the guides as a result of the accident. So, we continue on for a short distance to a large flat rocky surface—here we stop for lunch. The porters, who have gone before us, have a tent set up for us by the time we arrive.

As we drop our packs and wash our hands in a small pail of water by the food tent, the temperature begins to drop and clouds start settling around us creating a relatively dense fog. As we are eating, Nickson offers to split us into two groups, if some wish to make a detour on to Lava Tower before heading to Barranco Camp. Four members of the group, Tim, Carey, Christian, and Scott decide to make the detour. "This will be our only chance to ever see it," one of them says.

Leo, Vince, and I have no interest in extending today's journey. We still have at least three, maybe four, hours to go as it is before reaching this evening's camp. With the fog and the possibility of rain, we decide to stay the course. As the others are eating, I realize I have no appetite whatsoever; in fact, the sight of food seems almost repulsive to me. I sit and drink a cup or two of hot tea.

As we leave our lunch site, Nickson takes the others to the left toward Lava Tower. The rest of us follow Freddie down through a series of zigzags into a wide gulley where we cross two streams.

For the first time on our climb, it is beginning to rain. We stop and quickly pull ponchos from our packs and slip them over us. My poncho is a thin, lightweight gray garment with a large hood. It covers my head and my backpack and hangs to just below my knees. It is perfect for keeping my clothes and the items in my pack from getting soaked.

I do fine for a time, but once the trail begins another series of descents, the parka becomes my plague. It billows out in such a way that I cannot see my feet as I climb. This is not a problem on level ground or when we were ascending. However, once we start down into what seems to be an endless series of small valleys and gullies, I cannot see where to put one foot after the other. The lower part of the poncho completely obstructs my vision of the ground. To further complicate the situation, the hood slides over much of my face as I lean forward. Suddenly, this part of the trek becomes very difficult and slow. I gather my poncho in one hand and hold the hood steady with the other as I slowly find my footing, step after step.

Finally after about an hour and 40 minutes of difficult, wet, and slippery going, the rain lets up and we began a long descent into the Barranco Valley. The scenery is suddenly surreal. The hillsides, still shrouded in patches of fog, display large stands of senecio and tall lobelia. This valley is a thousand feet deep in some places. It was formed when a huge landslide swept southward from the upper reaches of the mountain several thousand years ago.

At about 4:15, Vince, Leo, and I finally make our way into camp. The sky begins to clear as we store our bags in our tents. We are in a high, narrow valley with a large slope on our right to the west. That is the way from which we have come. Below us is a grand vista; it is the most stunning view thus far. The African plains are thousands of feet below us. Behind us is a spectacular view of the summit's southwestern face. As we look at the summit, we can see to the left the outline of the Western Breach wall and the mighty Heim Glacier—breathtaking. It is a huge towering mass of gray-blue ice that has been chiseled by the wind.

To our east is another overwhelming sight. Rising just before us is a towering wall of rock. "We have to go over that wall tomorrow," Leo says.

"No way," I reply. "Are you sure?"

"Yes. It's called the Barranco Wall and we have to get on the other side of it to reach Barafu Camp."

My heart sinks. "I'll never make it," I think to myself quietly. There has already been more climbing than I thought we would encounter. I anticipated a more or less steep, but smooth, routine of daily trekking. For some reason I did not anticipate that there would be much actual vertical climbing. I now know I was wrong, very wrong. Today was the most difficult day so far, and now this, this towering wall. I feel a knot in my stomach.

The terrain just before us is much more rugged than anything we have seen or experienced to this point. Not only will the climbing be more difficult, but I am also aware that things are about to get more dangerous. We are going to have to contend with the serious risk of falling. To break a leg out here would be very grave, for the only medical help is several days walk away. I suppose a team of porters would have to carry an injured person back down the mountain, but that would be a long, painful, arduous journey. No wonder less than half of those who start the climb reach the summit.

Added to the risk of altitude sickness and the normal range of scrapes, bruises, bumps, cuts, and abrasions that accompany such an undertaking is the ever-present possibility of malaria, yellow fever, dysentery, hypothermia, and frostbite; each climber must now be extra careful. The IMAX film made it look so easy!

Finally, the sky is clear. The rest of our group has made it to camp and we are gathering for supper. The landscape is filled with the palette of a great painter. Rays of purple, red, and golden light streak across the sky as the sun bows its head to say farewell to another day.

Our evening meal is a more animated affair than usual. The members of our group who went on the Lava Tower have to work hard to convince Leo, Vince, and me that it was worth it. No one mentions the challenge that awaits us just outside the tent—the great wall is held at bay by simply not mentioning it, at least until Nickson and Freddie appear for their nightly visit and briefing. They describe the difficulty of the climb in very realistic terms and encourage us to rest well and be mentally ready for the challenge of tomorrow.

My steps are heavy as I walk back to the tent. In the far distance below I can see the lights of the town of Arusha in the distance. I know these lights are electric, but they look to me like the light of a thousand campfires. Perhaps this is because it has turned cold here on the mountain and we have no fire. Our only source of warmth is to bury ourselves back into our canvas cocoons. Who knows, perhaps tomorrow we will emerge as butterflies able to cross the Barranco Wall with ease.

I turn my vision and thoughts to the heavens. It is remarkably clear tonight; with each passing day we draw closer to the stars. Reaching my tent, I stoop to pull off my boots and scoot in backward for another night. It feels so good to stretch out. I slide into the sleeping bag and zip it tightly around me.

PRAYER

O God of time and timelessness, I thank You for these days of difficult struggle on this mountain. But I confess it is hard to be thankful. I am in a difficult place tonight. The trip is not pleasant, and I now doubt my physical stamina and strength of will to continue, and yet, I do have a strong sense that You are here with me. Help me, please, help me. Amen.

10
THE WALL
KARANGA CAMP

You always pass failure on the way to success.
—Mickey Rooney

Overnight: Karanga Camp (13,800 feet)

The morning sky begins to glow as the sun chins itself on the horizon. As the light strikes my tent, I realize I have been awake for a while, not wanting to admit it. To be awake is to know what is coming, and I am not ready to face another day. Nonetheless, I stir a bit, pull myself out of the sleeping bag, and begin to think through the clothes I will need for today. Surprisingly, I feel pretty good. I am so thankful that amid all of the rigors of this experience, I can sleep soundly.

I hear the porters now moving throughout our small encampment.

"Good morning, John."

"Hello, Ronald," I reply as I lean forward to unzip the front of the tent.

"I have water for your hands and hot tea."

"Thank you, Ronald, you are taking good care of us."

Journal: *Friday, January 27*

So here I am, sitting at Barranco Camp, looking out the flap of my tent. The sky is a pale clear blue. Walking yesterday was tough. In addition to the rain and fog, the altitude is beginning to take its toll—I was often breathless and weak. As I begin to dress for the day and repack my bag, I realize how stiff and sore I am from sleeping on the ground these past few days. I remind myself to be sure to stretch well before taking off again.

Today we face what is clearly going to be the most significant challenge of the trip thus far. We have to climb what is called the Great Barranco Wall. It is unusual for climbers to have to scale this massive wall, but because we are still moving laterally around the mountain, positioning ourselves to make an assault on the summit by a route other than the one planned, we must scale this huge ridgeline. I am more than a little worried about how I will do today, and I know the toughest stretch still lies ahead in another day or two, once we turn straight up toward the summit.

Oh, how I wish all of this was over. But it is not, and it will not be over for some time yet. I have no choice. I am absolutely stuck in this situation. I can't get out of it, and I don't want to continue. What we have come through these past few days is only a prelude for the real climb, which begins today.

But tomorrow will wait, and I need to let it wait. I can't face today and tomorrow at the same time. Today our plan is to intersect, on the other side of the wall, the south summit circuit that will take us to Karanga Camp, located about halfway between the Umbwe Route and the Mweka Route.

Everyone is subdued at breakfast. I still have no appetite. Carey is watching me to see if I am eating. When I do little more than take a few small bites, she says, "John is not eating." Tim encourages me to at least take a few more bites. I do my best, but the food just won't go down. I take a few orange slices and drink my coffee.

After breakfast, we are told to collapse our walking poles and strap them on our backs. We will not need them, nor can we use them once we reach the face of the wall. We quietly prepare. Everyone seems undone by the challenge just before us. There is no idle chatter. I am about to find out if I can meet this challenge.

Once we are ready, Joachim takes the lead, with Nickson

and Freddie positioning themselves among us so that everyone is within a person or two of a guide. Slowly we move down and out of camp toward the wall. At the base of the wall we must cross a small stream. It is wider and more rapid than the others we have crossed. Carefully we step along the rocks protruding out of the rushing water. To fall, at this point, could be very bad. Not only is injury a possibility, but also the prospect of falling fully into the water and thus becoming soaked from head to toe is daunting. Climbing this section with wet, slippery clothing would be almost impossible. One by one, with a helpful hand from our guides, we make it to the far side of the water.

What comes next, as we start the long climb straight up, turns out to be even more difficult than I had imagined. As I start the climb, I tell myself, "If they can do it, I can do it." But about a third of the way up the face of the wall, I can barely take one step after the next, pulling myself upward, stretching to get a handhold, and leaning into the face of the rock to keep my balance. "Just take the next step," I keep telling myself.

As I continue to climb, I do my best to forget about the height of the wall and concentrate on what is just before me. Often I need both hands to pull myself to where I can get a narrow foothold. I dare not look down.

"How are you doing, John?" Freddie calls to me from just above.

"Not well, this is really tough."

"Take a minute to catch your breath, you can make it."

I steady myself for a few moments and then begin again hauling my way, almost straight up, through thick vegetation and sharp volcanic edges. Time and again, I think I must be nearly to the top, only to realize there is much more to go. Each time this happens, my spirits sink and my strength seems to dissipate all the more.

Finally, I stop.

I just cannot go on. I am in trouble in a place where there is no room for trouble. The margin for error here is nil. I am little more than halfway up the face of the wall, but my energy and confidence are gone. I can't go up and I can't climb down.

Just then Scott pulls himself past me.

"Are you OK?" he asks.

"I don't know, Scott. I don't think I can make this."

A moment later, Freddie appears from up above. "John, it's me, Freddie. How you doing?"

"Not good," I say in a shallow voice.

I am not moving—just holding on, breathing slowly. Freddie calmly begins to take charge. "Give me your pack," he says. That hits me hard, for to give my pack to someone else to carry is to admit my weakness in a very open and obvious way. Part of the code of the climb is that everyone must carry his or her own weight; yet here I am unable to go on.

But after a few more moments, I slowly slip off my backpack and Freddie slings it over his shoulder. He now must carry his pack and mine. He pats me on the arm as he says quietly, "It's all right, John, we'll do this together. Just put your foot right here."

With his encouragement giving me strength, I take a step, then another, and another. Without the weight of the pack, the climbing seems a little easier, and with each step, a small measure of hope takes root. Up and up, back and forth, we go for nearly 45 minutes when I hear Freddie say, "We're almost there." I don't yet let myself believe it.

Somehow, with Freddie's help, I finally pull myself up onto a large flat area at the top of the wall. All of the others are already there, waiting. I am so glad to see them and, yet, embarrassed as well. They have had to wait on me. My whole life is about leadership, but now I can barely follow. My ego now aches more than my legs and shoulders. However, no one seems smug as I struggle to find a place to sit down. It has been hard for everyone.

As I think back over that part of the journey, there are two things that come to mind. First is the vivid imagery of help coming from above. In the midst of my trouble, when I could go no further, a guide comes to me, calls me by name, and assures me I am not alone in this moment of distress. He comforts me and takes the burden I am carrying and makes it his own. Then, putting a hand on my shoulder, this one from above says, "Follow me, together we can make."

It was a God-moment for me.

This was an example of how individuals are to make the journey of life together. We are to bear one another's burdens, go to the person in need, offer comfort and assistance. How often, on my way to the top, do I slip past a person who is in trouble?

The second thing that lodges in my mind and heart as I think about Barranco Wall was the reaction of the other climbers when I finally appeared on the small plateau at the top. No one was critical of my shortcoming; no one made fun of me. No one said, "You don't belong on this trip." It was one of the moments that transformed us from strangers to friends.

Journal: *From the top of Barranco Wall to Karanga Camp*

We take about 15 minutes to rest and drink as much water as we can. This break gives me a few minutes to write these lines. The view from the top of the wall is breathtaking, yet we have little breath to spare. The sky is clear above us. We can see the summit of Kilimanjaro towering on high, with the great Heim Glacier over our shoulders to the north. The line at the summit, where the ice meets the sky, is a jagged sharp white edge against the bright blue.

Below stretches a wide rugged valley. We can see the trail extending in front of us. It appears to be essentially a long gentle descent into the western part of the Karanga Valley. Stretched out below the mountain, we look down upon a quilt of clouds starting to blanket the lowlands.

Soon, too soon, we will be back on our feet to descend down the sloping backside of the ridge. At our present altitude we can see below and above us the changing landscape—ferns, heather, and other greenery begins to reappear as we move back down for a time.

More later . . .

Making our way down into the valley, there are two more streams to cross before we come to a flat gravel area, where we stop for lunch. I continue to have no appetite; in fact, the sight of food now makes me ill. I force myself to eat a few bites and drink as much water as I can get down.

To the east is a path that snakes toward a high pass—this means another climb. I think our next camp is just beyond the ridge. Although this section will mean more vertical ascent, it does not appear to be nearly as difficult as what we faced this morning.

I try to stay in the moment and to notice the shapes and colors, feel the textures, and smell the smells. I also am becoming increasingly aware of the weather. How did it come to be that the phrase "talking about the weather" means talking about nothing important or nothing in particular? A person has only to imagine the magnitude and variety and power of weather to see what a source of wonder and revelation it is. It is an ever potent presence on the mountain. It is a force over which we have no control, and because we are deep into the wilderness, its impact on us is immediate and personal—there is no place to run or hide.

Such a trip causes a person to focus on the present moment;

one becomes very connected to the now. As we begin the ascent up out of the valley toward our next campsite, I am beginning to realize in a personal way the value of an attentive heart—being open to God at each step along the mountain. The novelist Henry Miller once observed: "The moment one gives close attention to anything, even a blade of grass, it becomes a mysterious, awesome, indescribably magnificent world in itself."[12]

After another hour and a half, we crest the ridgeline and see the tents beyond us. Fifteen minutes more and we are there! Tonight we camp on a small flat plateau about two-thirds of the way between Barranco Camp and Barafu. This place is called Karanga Camp. The topography is rugged and sparse. Above us the peak is clear. It is a magnificent sight that, in spite of fears and fatigue, continues to draws us upward.

In spite of all of the ups and downs of the day and the two major ascents, we have not gained much altitude. Our goal was to move laterally, rather than vertically, to position ourselves to reach Barafu Camp relatively early in the day tomorrow. That will be our final staging area for the ascent to the summit.

At dinner, everyone is quiet. Tim's feet are continuing to be a source of significant pain and discomfort. He is vigilant, nonetheless. He does not complain, but we can tell that the trip is exceedingly difficult for him. Vince and Leo remain in good spirits, even bantering a bit about who should take the last helping of pasta. Christian is quiet. I huddle inside my jacket at the end of the table.

At the end of the meal, Nickson and Freddie stop in to talk about the climb tomorrow. They assure us that tomorrow will be an easier day. We will move to Barafu Camp. We set the time for departure at 8:30 A.M. instead of an earlier time. This means a little more sleep tonight!

On the short walk back to my tent, I find the Southern Cross once more and stop to pray for God's protection and help. The temperature is falling fast. The sky is clear and the mountain around me looks brittle in the light of the moon and stars. The night is very still, and I feel as though I am a million light-years away from home.

I am so glad to edge my way back into the tent and begin to settle in for the night. I am completely exhausted. I slip into the sleeping bag still fully dressed, except for my shoes. I need the clothes for added warmth, but I also have no energy or desire to change. My hat is pulled down over my ears as I lay my head on my backpack. I leave the flashlight on for a while. I want to sleep; but at the same time, I know that once I go to sleep, the next thing I know it will be another difficult day.

PRAYER

Guide me now, O gentle God, into a time of rest. Ease my spirit through the presence of Your Spirit. Calm my fears, quiet my racing and anxious thoughts. Let me, with each breath, let go of the heaviness I feel. Let the deep darkness just outside my tent be a source of comfort rather than fear. Tomorrow, may I have the strong steady sense that I am walking arm-in-arm with You. Give me an added sense of assurance that You are here on the mountain. Open my eyes to see You on the trail, to hear You in the wind, feel You through the rays of sun or in the mist. You, alone, are my strength and shield and my salvation. Amen.

11

KEEP LOOKING UP
BARAFU CAMP

Adversity introduces a man to himself.
—Anonymous

Overnight: Barafu Camp (16,100 feet)

Journal: *Saturday, January 28*

    Today we are scheduled to take a short hike from Karanga up a steep boulder-strewn path to Barafu Camp. The weather there is often windy and constantly changing, with snow squalls and freezing temperatures. Barafu means "ice" in Swahili. The name is given to the place because of its proximity to the Rebmann Glacier, which sits off to the northwest. Here the wild earth of long ago lives on.

    Hans Meyer, the first European to climb Kilimanjaro, noted in his journal that, "Camp life on Kilimanjaro is a school for the practice of self-denial." I am working on my attitude and outlook. In reality, every day of the climb has been fascinating. I keep saying to myself, "I've never seen anything like this." I think back to the first day as we walked through the forest—that was fascinating. Then we broke out into the higher heath land with its many flowers and breathtaking views and I thought, "Nothing can top this." But now, looking up from this vantage point, I see a new splendor—an austere beauty. By tonight, we will be within striking distance of the summit of Kilimanjaro.

    Above 14,000 feet one enters a harsher world; the wind is strong and the temperatures begin to drop significantly as the heat from the plains fully dissipates, though the sun's rays remain

113

intense. I know that today will not be an easy day. Though we are not scheduled to travel very far, perhaps only five hours of walking, and yet, I have a feeling that because of the altitude and the increasing incline, this will be a taxing day.

Because we are at the equator, there is a clear rhythm to the day. It gets dark every evening at 6 P.M. and light every morning at 6 A.M. It is morning, just now, but I have not yet gone for breakfast. I am sure that Ronald will come by soon to see if I am awake. It is nice to have a few quiet moments before setting out. I am still sick, but I am feeling OK—does that makes any sense? I think I am just getting used to being nauseated.

Gathering for breakfast as usual, the food has begun to all look and smell the same. I assume it tastes the same as well, though I am still not eating. All the food we have on the trip is carried by the porters from our starting point down the mountain. As the days wear on, the fresh nature of the food declines, yet the overall nature of our meals remains constant and good, considering the challenges of this climb.

Spirits seem pretty high this morning. Scott is very talkative. He is always pleasant but generally does not lead in the conversation. Following the meal, the routine is the same: back to the tent to pack up our gear and make sure our supplies for the day are in order. As we leave Karanga Camp, Freddie is leading the way, then Scott, Christian, Tim, Carey, Vince, me, and Leo. We leave the cleanup and the tear-down of camp to the faithful porters who must repack everything and carry it on to the next campsite. We are very careful to not leave anything behind— any garbage or trash.

As we continue to climb, we gain a greater sense of the life of the mountain itself. Kilimanjaro produces its own, self-contained, self-sustained ecosystem. Anyone climbing the mountain becomes aware that this ecosystem is made up of altitudinal layers, reflected in the vegetation as well as temperature, rainfall, and thinning atmosphere. At the beginning of the climb, moving from the dry savanna and thorn scrub of the plains, you pass first through a cultivated zone to reach the mountain forest, the level from which most trekking routes start. The forest can be divided into rain forest and cloud forest before it gives way to the alpine zones above. These are rich in vegetation at first but become increasingly barren as the elevation increases. Then comes the glaciers and the summit icecap.

As plants and flowers fade from our path, the terrain seems lifeless and yet there is still the mountain itself. Being a volcano puts Kilimanjaro in an elite cadre among the world's great mountains. Whether extinct, dormant, or still active, volcanoes are tied to the inner life of the earth, as though the smoke and lava are breath and blood. This connection with the deep makes the mountain seem alive. The higher we go, the more I sense the power buried beneath my feet.

There seems to be a new sense of reward as I now walk on this high slope. It is counterintuitive, but great progress can be made by simply putting one foot in front of the other. Much of life comes down to taking the next step and letting the small things add up over time. No one reaches the summit in one sprint or one giant step. Instant success isn't instant. Progress comes gradually at the price of consistent effort in the same direction.

As we begin to reach these upper altitudes, I am particularly mindful of the symptoms and dangers of altitude sickness:

Acute Mountain Sickness (AMS)—The most common altitude-related problem is acute mountain sickness, which is caused by ascending to high elevations too quickly to adjust. AMS can set in at altitudes as low as 8,000 feet but becomes more likely once a climber crosses the 12,500-foot mark.

Symptoms of AMS include headache, breathlessness, nausea, vomiting, dizziness, a rasping cough, insomnia, and a loss of appetite and energy. This condition is occasionally hard to identify because many (most) climbers who live at lower altitudes will experience some measure of all of these symptoms. If, however, the symptoms persist, the only treatment is to immediately descend to a lower altitude, then rest.

High-Altitude Pulmonary Edema (HAPE)—This condition is caused by an accumulation of fluid in the lungs and can come on quickly and kill a victim within a few hours. Added to many of the symptoms of AMS are chest pain, a gurgling noise in the chest, and a cough with bloody sputum. The best treatment is to get the individual to a lower elevation as soon as possible, even if it means carrying the person. If oxygen is available, it can be administered to aid the victim as he or she descends.

High-Altitude Cerebral Edema (HACE) is the most serious altitude-related illness and is caused by severe lack of oxygen. The large and small arteries of the brain dilate so that they can carry more blood and more oxygen, causing the brain to swell. One of the obvious results of this swelling is a tremendous headache. Other symptoms include confusion, hallucination, an inability to control emotions, and a staggering walk.

One of the most important rules for making it to the top is to pay attention to your body. To help counter the risk of altitude sickness, I have been cautioned to climb slowly and drink lots of water. One of the advantages of the longer Western Breach route is that it allows more time to adjust to the altitude. So far, everyone seems to be coping well. I do sense my breathing is more rapid, and I have to stop frequently to just catch my breath.

There is a stop about midmorning for a water break and then around noon we stop again for lunch. We drop our packs. There is no place to pitch a tent or duck in out of the wind and sun; we have learned to just lean back against the rocks to rest and eat. The meal looks pretty meager. I feel like trying to eat, so I take some orange slices and bread, but they are hard to swallow and I end up not eating very much. However, I am able to drink quite a bit of water and almost immediately I can feel the difference it makes. I must continually remind myself to keep drinking.

We are now above 15,000 feet and the sky is clear. From our vantage point we can see great stretches of open land far below us, particularly to the southwest. Here, there is also a wondrous view of Kilimanjaro's smaller peak, Mawenzi, off to our right. It is rugged and displays the light and shadows in patterns that seem to magnify its uneven profile.

The afternoon walk passes uneventfully. We reach Barafu Camp relatively early. Once we get our things in our tents, we have a couple of hours to rest before our evening meal. Vince, Leo, Freddie, and I sit together for a while to simply take in the view.

We are now above 16,000 feet. It is cold and barren. Until now, the terrain where we have camped has been mostly level, but here there is no level ground near us; so the porters have pitched our tents and set up camp on the high slope. This living on a slant adds to the moderate disorientation we are experiencing because of the altitude.

We are at the base of the final ascent to the summit. At this height, we have about half of the oxygen that is present at sea level, and we still have to climb over 3,000 feet nearly straight up. There is a growing sense of anxiety as we look up at the peak, which is just before us.

Tomorrow will be the day when we push ourselves to reach the crater wall. We will leave in darkness headed for a breach in the wall known as Stella Point. I can't let myself think about it, and yet I can't quit thinking about it. Freddie senses that we are nervous.

"Tomorrow you will stand on the floor of the great volcano," he says with the confidence we are lacking.

"How tough will it be tomorrow?" Leo asks.

"Well, it will not be easy. Nothing is easy on the mountain," Freddie replies. "The secret is to go slowly," he continues.

"*Pole, pole,*" I say in Swahili.

"Yes, slowly, slowly," he replies. "Just keep going. We will reach the crater rim and then descend into the volcano for rest."

"When Tanzania was granted its independence in 1961, a great torch was lit on the summit," Freddie tells us with pride. "President Julius Nyerere said that the Uhuru Torch was a symbol of the rebirth of Tanzania; its light was to shine beyond our borders giving hope where there was despair, love where there was hate, and dignity where before there was only humiliation."

Julius Kambarage Nyerere was born on April 13, 1922, in Butiama, on the eastern shore of Lake Victoria in northwest Tanzania. His father was the chief of the small Zanaki tribe. He was 12 before he started school. Later, he transferred for his secondary education to the Tabora Government Secondary School. His intelligence was quickly recognized by the Roman Catholic fathers who taught him. He went on, with their help, to train as a teacher at Makerere University in Kampala (Uganda). On gaining his teaching certificate, he taught for three years and then went on a government scholarship to study history and political economics for his master of arts at the University of Edinburgh. He was the first Tanzanian to study at a British university and only the second to gain a university degree outside Africa. Nyerere's integrity, ability as a political orator and organizer, and readiness to work with different groups was a significant factor in achieving independence without bloodshed.

As we listen to Freddie talk about the history of his country and its present challenges, I sense his pride and also his desire that Tanzania might continue to develop into a great nation. "Tomorrow," he says once more. "Tomorrow." At this point I am not sure if he is thinking of tomorrow as it refers to our climb to the crater or to his climb, along with his people, to a better day as a nation.

We sit quietly for a time. Then, as we begin to feel the chill, we scatter to our tents to get out of the weather and rest awhile. Soon Ronald wakes me from my nap and lets me know supper is ready. We gather in a sacrament fashion at the table. There is by now a sense of ritual, a thanksgiving and a communal break-ing of bread that takes place at the end of each day. As far as I can tell, I am the only one who takes time to offer a silent prayer, yet I sense a certain reverence in the group. Tonight we are gathered on the eve of something very special.

Following a meal of rice and vegetables, we receive our nightly briefing from Nickson and Freddie. They remind us that we will get up at 4 A.M. and will leave camp in the dark, around 5:00. Nickson wraps up our time together by saying, "You should plan on eight or nine hours of climbing to reach Stella Point, on the crater rim. There we will rest and then descend in-to the crater for camp."

In silence, we file out and disperse to our separate tents. I just want to get some sleep. I don't want to think any more about tomorrow. I stop long enough to look up and see the heavens above me. This sight is truly astonishing. It is as if God has pulled back the curtains so that all the lights of heaven shine through. The sky has great depth and texture with varied shades of light.

PRAYER

Praise belongs to You, O God, who spins the shining stars across the heavens, who lifts the dawn into place and sets boundaries for the night, who awes the earth with storms and gentles it with breezes. I thank You tonight for the sweat of the journey, which just keeps getting harder. I think I am finally growing stronger in spirit and determination, thanks to Your keeping grace. Tomorrow will be a great test. Watch over me and give me strength, in Jesus' name. Amen.

12
THE SUMMIT!
CRATER CAMP

The heights by great men reached and kept were not attained
by sudden flight, but they, while their companions slept,
were toiling upward in the night.
—Henry Wadsworth Longfellow

Overnight: Crater Camp (18,750 feet)

Journal: *Sunday, January 29*

The world is silent and still as I lie between earth and heaven, which now seem quite close. Icy fingers of snow reach into my tent. I check the time; it is about 4:00 in the morning. I can hear the porters moving about. We are scheduled to be up and out within the next half-hour or so to begin the day in darkness.

We'll leave before first light (about 5 A.M.) and ascend nearly 3,000 feet up to the crater wall. That will take five to six hours followed by another 50 minutes or so to our camp, which is set in the wide crater of Kili's summit amid the indigo-streaked Furtwangler Glacier, in an arctic moonscape.

Today presents the toughest challenge of the entire climb because of the steep vertical slope and the high altitude and thin air. Our trek will require an extra measure of stamina and determination. It will test not only our physical abilities but the strength of our minds and hearts as well. Only time will tell if we have what it takes to reach the heights. I am very excited about this challenge.

I am still in the sleeping bag. It is warm in here, and I know that it is very cold outside. I will stay just a few minutes more to make these notes, pray for today, and reflect. These early morning moments are a valuable investment in the rest of the day.

I pull myself out of the sleeping bag; I am still fully dressed from the day before, except for my coat and shoes. I slip on my coat and pack my bag, making sure I have my water bottles and notes; scooting to the end of the tent I slowly unzip the flap. Cold air rushes in. The others are up. I hear Vince and Leo talking. I pull on my boots, grab my gloves, and slip out of my tent. I am just a little dizzy as I stand up. So I hold steady for a moment and then begin to walk toward the breakfast tent.

Poking my head in, I move slowly around the table to take a seat on the other side. Tim and Carey follow, then Christian and Scott. We are all here. Ronald comes in to bring us hot water for coffee or tea. I am still nauseated. The sight and smell of food is almost more than I can stand. I have no sense of hunger at all; and it has been over three days since I had a full meal.

Last night I tried once more to eat an energy bar that Carey had given me. I could only take three or four bites. I know this lack of food cannot go on, and yet I just cannot make myself eat.

Tim notices that I am just sitting there. "Hey, John, today is going to be the toughest day of all. You have to eat something. Just try."

"Thanks, Tim. I know you are right, I just can't get it down."

I dish up a few scoops of scrambled eggs and take some orange slices. The orange is pretty good, but I can only get about half of the eggs down. I drink some coffee and watch the others refill their plates.

Nickson pops his head in the tent. "We leave in 10 minutes."

Soon we are gathered at the edge of the camp. It is still dark. We are wearing headlamps, which will light our path. All senses are alert—every nuance of my being is finely tuned. Off we go, "*pole, pole.*" What will this day bring?

The climb is long and demanding; by far this is the toughest day yet. My legs are tired, and we have just begun. My lungs twinge, my throat is dry, my lips are cracked, my stomach is upset, my back hurts, and my head aches. With each step, the climb is getting very steep. I am increasingly breathless. It is just 45 minutes into today's climb, and I am already exhausted. Though all these things are true, I am doing pretty well. My spirit is strong, and my determination has returned. I remind myself that life is ultimately lived from the inside out, rather than the outside in.

As we begin to reach the top of Kibo, I realize in a personal way that this mountain is a volcano. Near the crater rim we begin to smell the strong scent of warm sulfur seeping from deep within the mountain. The idea of spending the night on the floor of the crater is one filled with wonder and fear. We are very high, nearing 18,000 feet, where the air is thin and the wind is cold; it takes great strength of will to keep walking.

Behind me I can hear Freddie, our guide, singing. The song is familiar in a way, but I can't make it out. "Freddie, what are you singing?" I call to him. Rather than answer me directly, he just starts singing all the louder. It is then that I can make out the words to his song. It is an old Jimmy Buffett song, called "Volcano." The lyrics picture a volcano erupting, lava and all.

"Thanks, Freddie, we needed that!" I reply.

We are looking straight up now into a bright blue sky. The sun shoots splinters of light off the snow-covered summit. Immediately before me, however, I can see nothing more than the few steps and handholds. I feel as though I cannot keep going, and yet I cannot quit; so I do what a person must do in such moments—I just keep walking, one difficult step following the other.

Suddenly, as I lift myself over a rock ledge, I am there, at the rim of the crater! This is Stella Point. There is a rush of emotion, relief, exhilaration, and awe. Stretching out before and just below me is the wide expanse of the floor of the volcanic crater and several massive glaciers standing four to five stories high.

Tim, who has been just ahead of me, pulls me up and beams as he says—"We've made it. We're here!" Sitting down and leaning against the inside of the crater wall, the others join us, one by one.

We begin taking pictures and give ourselves time to let our heart rates slow. The air is noticeably dryer; we begin to drink an added measure of water. While we are resting, Nickson points out a spot well below us, out on the edge of the crater floor, where we will make camp tonight. The plan is to sleep there overnight and then push on to the peak in the morning.

However, as we are sitting together, resting, someone in the group says, "Let's keep going! The peak is not that far; we are so close."

Several agree immediately. I thought it would be particularly meaningful to stand at the summit on Sunday. We ask Nickson about going on. "Are you serious?" he asks in disbelief.

"Yes!"

"Do you realize it will mean at least another hour or more of extremely hard trekking? The terrain is steep, snowy, and treacherous because of the loose volcanic rock."

Nonetheless, buoyed by the prospect of reaching the summit today, we all agree to venture on. Once more we lift our packs, grab our poles, and with Nickson in the lead, begin the final ascent. Actually, the climb itself is not too difficult, apart from one or two areas where we have to climb up and over various large rock formations. We can only walk a short distance without stopping to breathe and regain our strength. We are nearing 19,000 feet. The summit is just before us in the distance; we see the silhouette of the rough wooden sign that marks the spot.

Step by step, leaning hard on our poles, watching our feet and concentrating just enough to take one step after the next, we begin to draw close. We pause for one more brief rest. As we begin once more, someone behind me says in a strong voice, "Let John go first, it's Sunday." So, I move out a few steps ahead of the group and lift myself up the last few feet to touch the sign.

I turn slowly to make a 360-degree rotation. The rim of the crater extends out in a large circle at my feet; the bowl of volcano is nearly 1,000 feet lower and out in the distance far below is the wide expanse of the continent itself.

I turn and look into the frozen faces of my friends. It is quiet; a sense of reverence has encompassed us all. I lift my arms to the sky and quote from Ps. 19, "The heavens declare the glory of God; and the firmament sheweth his handywork" (v. 1, KJV).

"Surely we have experienced the reality of this verse," and then . . . without warning, I begin to weep. A flood of emotion pours forth from deep within. I am exhausted and exhilarated, tired and triumphant, relieved and inspired in the same moment. I step away from the summit, and one by one my companions make their final ascent.

We take pictures and laugh and congratulate one another. As I stand to the side and watch each one at the summit, I think of the quotation, "Oh! I have slipped the surly bonds of earth . . . and touched the face of God."[13] This is as close as I will get.

Our next task is to walk back down the rim of the volcano onto the floor of the wide crater where we will camp tonight. The descent into the crater proves to be a tricky trek. The interior walls of the rim are steep and covered with loose volcanic gravel. I find I must move very slowly, supported by my poles, as I make my way downward in a broad, serpentine pattern.

The crater has the feel of a primeval place. It is decidedly inhospitable and barren and yet invites us to come closer. Finally I arrive at the floor of the crater. Flat land at last! In the distance I can see our tents set against the backdrop of a massive glacier. What a sight.

My legs are weak and my breathing is slow and labored as I walk the last few yards to camp. It is very cold, and I am so stiff. I turn to look back at the summit. It stands at attention, seemingly out of respect for those of us who have just come to call.

Once I reach my tent, I make my way in and stretch out on the mat. I just want to stay right here. I doze off for about 40 minutes or so, then I hear the call of the porters to our evening meal. The idea of food is repulsive to me. Not only can I not eat, but I don't even want to see food; yet I go to sit at the table. No one says much. The small candle on the middle of the table just barely holds a flame, the oxygen is so low.

"How are you doing, Christian?" I ask. He looks my way, but it does not seem to register that I have asked him a question. He says nothing. "Well, we made it, I can't believe we made it," I say in his general direction. No response. He is really wiped out, I think to myself.

As soon as the meal is ended, we file out one by one to our tents. All of us just want to get warm and try to sleep. I slip off my shoes and zip the sleeping bag around me. I still have on all my clothes, including my coat, hat, and gloves.

One of the things that enters my mind tonight as I lie on this high bed of stone is the contrast between life viewed from within the tent compared to the view one gets from the wide expanse of the high mountain. We need both. There is a centering that takes place in solitude and quiet. I have already learned that strength for the day begins with prayer, reflection, and a careful thinking of the challenges awaiting me on that particular day's climb.

A person notices things when he or she walks step by step—no speed, up close—hands-on. Kilimanjaro's treasures and secrets are revealed slowly. Georgia O'Keeffe wrote:

Nobody sees a flower, really—it's so small—we haven't time, and to see takes time. Many people miss much of the beauty and wonder of daily life because they live at such a hurried pace with little time to reflect and see.

We are starving for moments of solitude . . . Our starvation deprives us of the nutrition that those in-between times used to give us: a feeling of centeredness in our lives, awareness of our spiritual needs and those of our families, a confident sense of self-knowledge.[14]

Mother Teresa of Calcutta observed that "God cannot be found in noise and restlessness. God is the friend of silence."[15] For Mother Teresa, activity did not lead to God, silence did—but the God she encountered in those quiet moments led her (propelled her!) to a life of meaningful activity.

The reason for retreat is to advance; the reason for stopping is to get going. Silence clarifies and motivates. Marian Wright Edelman writes, "Learn to be quiet enough to hear the sound of the genuine within yourself so that you can hear it in others."[16] I love the silence of the mountain—in this silence I hear God.

I like a response that jazz musician Miles Davis made when asked about the intangibles of being a great musician. He said, "Don't play what's there, play what's not there." I understand him to be saying, to play the notes (what's there), but also pay attention to the music that transcends the notes. See what is there, but also what is not there. Hear what is said, but also listen for what is not said.

Tonight, in this barren place, all is quiet—yet much is said.

PRAYER

Dear God of silence as well as thunder, I know You are here on the mountaintop. I am literally sick and tired, and yet I am not in despair. I have reached a goal and stood where few have ever stood. Tonight I will sleep by a tower of ice in the heart of the tropics. I have once again been awed by the majesty and power of Your creation. You are amazing! The psalmist says it well:

> *Lord, you have been our dwelling place*
> *throughout all generations.*
> *Before the mountains were born*
> *or you brought forth the earth and the world,*
> *from everlasting to everlasting you are God.*
> —Ps. 90:1-2

Although I sleep on the roof of a great volcano, I will rest in You. I pray for my friends who take shelter in neighboring tents. Thank You for their companionship on this rigorous journey. Their presence has lightened my load. Give us rest and strength. Amen.

13

WHAT GOES UP . . .
MWEKA CAMP

Don't set your sights on the summit; set your sights on getting down.
—Mark Goldfain

Overnight: Mweka Camp (11,000 ft.)

Journal: *Monday, January 30*

What goes up must come down, and that includes us. Getting to the summit was optional, but now that I am here, getting down is mandatory.

Once more I awake to voices. I can tell it is light, but I just want to stay here, in this warm envelope. I am stiff; maybe I am frozen and don't know it yet. This has been another short night; although I seemed to have slept well . . . when I slept.

Last night as I first crawled into the tent and slid into my sleeping bag, my mind was racing with images from the summit. I can't believe I made it. I couldn't sleep at first. I was very tired, maybe too tired for slumber. And I just couldn't seem to get enough air. It was so cold.

Finally, I drifted off to sleep only to be awakened suddenly by voices and footsteps. We were alone; who could be up and walking about at this hour? I listened carefully but could not recognize the muted voices or discern the muffled conversation. I was too tired and too warm to even think of getting up to see what might be going on. After a time, the voices ceased and I slipped back into a restless, shallow sleep.

"Good morning, John."

"Hello, my friend. Is it time to get up?"

"Yes, we leave in less than an hour. Breakfast is ready."
"I will be right there."
As I stir in my tent, I notice that the water in the bottles at the sides of my backpack is frozen. No wonder I was cold last night!

The plan for today is to begin the descent via the Mweka Route back to Barafu Camp for lunch. Then we continue down the mountain to our final campsite nestled in thick heather on the southern slopes. I make my way out of the tent and step onto the lunar surface, or at least it seems that way. The terrain is bleak and desolate. "One small step for man . . . ," I say to myself.

The wind gusts cut like a thousand knife blades. My skin is dry, my breath is white. Nearly every part of me feels frozen. Once I arrive at the meal tent, I step in to find a somber group of hearty companions staring into their coffee cups. "Sunny and 70 again today," I say, trying to get a reaction. No one stirs. We are depleted of strength, stamina, and humor.

"What was all the commotion about in the night?" I ask.

"Tim and Christian got sick, really sick," Vince tells me. "It was altitude sickness and they were taken down in the night."

"What do you mean, taken down?"

"Nickson got them up and dressed and sent them with two of the porters to start walking down the mountain."

"In the dark?" I ask, trying to make sense of this.

"Yes, can you believe it?"

"Will they be all right?" I wonder out loud.

Just then Carey walks in. She had stayed with the group during the night rather than go with her husband, Tim. That must have been hard.

"Are you OK?"

"Yeah, I just want to get off this mountain," she replies.

"What happened?"

"Christian wasn't doing well at supper last night. Remember when you asked him a question and he just stared at you?"

"I thought he was just tired," I said.

"No, it was the beginning of the second stage of altitude sickness. When we got back to the tent, I could tell that Tim was also starting to fade. It scared me, so I called for Nickson and Freddie. Once they talked to Tim and checked on Christian, they decided not to take a chance by waiting until morning. So as soon as they were fully dressed again, two of the porters went with them and they started down. I stayed to care for all of our gear, plus there wasn't anything I could do."

"I am sorry, Carey," I said.

"Thanks, John. You can't imagine what it is like to watch your husband walk away into the night at 18,500 feet."

We finished our meal in silence. I ate a few slices of orange and tried my best to get some of the cereal down. I could only take about six or seven bites.

After breakfast, I walked back to my tent. I am moving slowly and breathing with difficulty. The sky, however, is clear and the sun is bright. I tell myself that this will be a good day; we are headed down.

Within a few minutes we are again underway, marching in single file across the barren landscape. We reach the crater rim after about 40 minutes of walking. There, we pause for water and for one last long look across the bowl of the crater with its towering glaciers. I will never see such a sight again.

Now, finally after seven days of climbing ever upward, we start down. The first phase will be to retrace our route from Barafu Camp. There we will stop for lunch and meet up with the porters who stayed behind with equipment and supplies we did not wish to carry to the summit. We also hope to catch up with Tim and Christian there at the camp.

After a few final instructions from Nickson, we head out over the crater rim and, assisted by gravity, begin the last leg of the journey, carrying with us the memory of our view from the summit and our night in the crater. The slope leading from the crater rim is steep and unstable. The descent begins with a wide swath of scree, which is pea-sized pumice that covers the upper slopes. This gives way ever so slightly downward with each step we take, so there is little sense of stability.

I can tell right way that this slip-sliding descent is going to take a toll on my knees. I use my poles to slow my pace and steady myself. Our group begins to spread out across the wide slope as we make our way down. I am with Leo and Vince. We make looping strides and occasionally break into a hop or slow, controlled run, like skiers with no skis. We are moving a little more slowly than the others. My spirits are beginning to pick up. To our left is the summit of Mawenzi, Kili's little sister. It is fully illuminated by the bright morning sun.

It continues to surprise me how physically difficult the descent is. How hard can it be to go downhill? Very hard!

We arrive back at Barafu Camp, having descended almost 3,000 feet in a three-and-half-hour walk. Lunch is ready, and we reconnect with Tim and Christian. They both seem to be doing well, given the difficult night they experienced. Following lunch we head out toward what will be our last campsite, Mweka Camp, which is set in the upper regions of the tree belt. We will descend all the way to just above 10,000 feet.

The trail heading from Barafu to Mweka is wide open. There is very little vegetation. From time to time, as we make our way downward, we have to scramble down over the rocks. After coming through one of those difficult stretches, perhaps an hour or so into the afternoon descent, I realize I am slowly falling behind the others. Vince and Leo have slowed down to stay with me, and Nickson is following some distance behind us, having left camp a bit later than the rest of us.

As we are walking down this gently sloping section, my legs suddenly give way, and before I know it, I am on the ground. Once I am down, I realize I had not stumbled but have passed out. I feel weak and faint. Fortunately, I have not hurt myself, but I cannot stand up. Vince and Leo lift me so I can lean against a rock. I take my water bottle and slowly begin to drink. In just a moment Nickson is here with me. I tell him I think I am all right, but I need some time to rest. He tells us there is a ranger station about 15 minutes farther below us on the trail. The sky is beginning to darken with storm clouds, so he suggests that I try to make it to the station where I can rest for a while.

He raises me up and I try to regain my sense of balance, but in spite of my best efforts, I can barely stand. "I really am washed out," I tell Nickson. As we stand there a moment, another man appears on the trail with us. Apparently, he is a guide with another group, although I have not seen any other climbers. Where did he come from right at this moment when I need help? I put one arm over his shoulder and the other arm around Nickson and with their support, we head out.

Within a few minutes, we see the tin roof of an old building at the ranger station in the distance. After another 10 to 15 minutes we stumble into this permanent outpost. Two rangers are there, sitting on a small bench outside one of the two dark green metal sheds. I rest for a few moments on another bench with Vince and Leo. Nickson carries on a conversation in Swahili with the rangers.

"It's going to rain hard in a few minutes," Nickson says. "Let's go inside."

With his assistance, I walk a few paces and enter a dark, starkly-furnished shelter. There is a set of bunk beds, a bench, a table, and a couple of oil lamps. There is also a shortwave radio hooked up to a small portable generator.

The stranger who met us a few moments ago on the trail is gone. "Where did he go?" I ask.

"Who?" Nickson asks.

"The other fellow."

"I don't know," he says. I can't tell if Nickson doesn't know where the fellow has gone or doesn't know what I am talking about.

Leo and Vince step in to ask how I am doing. I tell them I am OK, just a little weak. "Because it is going to rain soon, we are going to head out and try to make it to camp before we get soaked," Leo tells me.

"That's a good idea," I reply. "I'm OK."

Soon they are gone. Nickson, the rangers, and I sit in silence for another 15 minutes or so. A small handful of young Africans are hanging around the compound. They appear to be porters, or perhaps, would-be porters, hoping to encounter climbers in need of some assistance. After a time, one of rangers stirs and hands me a Coca-Cola. Amazing, here we are in the middle of nowhere and I am drinking a Coke.

Soon, the heavens open and a very heavy rain begins to pour down. I don't think Leo and Vince are going to make it without getting very wet. Fortunately, I am crowded into the little hut for shelter. The rain pounds the tin roof for the next hour or so, then finally dissipates.

Once it clears a bit, I tell Nickson that I think I am strong enough to continue, but he says he doesn't think I can make it by myself. What occurs next is still hard for me to believe. Nickson and three or four other porters from the group that have been just hanging around disappear for a moment and return to the front of the hut with a stretcher mounted on a very large center wheel. Evidently this is kept at the station to assist climbers who are injured. Nickson says to me, "We will take you to the camp on this." I am not sure this is necessary, but I don't seem to have the energy or will to refuse.

As I lay myself onto the sloping stretcher, Nickson covers me with a blanket and then ties me onto the stretcher/gurney with a rope that loops around and across from my chest to my knees. Two porters grab the handles near my head and tip me backward, raising me to a flat position, suspended over the large wheel. The others take hold of the handles near my feet.

Off we go, bouncing, tilting, and turning our way downward. I feel every bump. The rope holding me on the gurney is so tight I can't move to adjust myself to the jostling of the journey. I finally just close my eyes and pretend I am on a bad ride at an amusement park that will soon be over. It takes a little more than an hour for us to reach camp.

Upon arrival, the rest of the group gathers around me as though viewing the body at a wake.

"Can you believe this?" I ask Scott.

"Are you OK?" he asks.

"I think so; I just passed out, but I'm OK."

After getting my picture taken three or four times while still tied to the stretcher, I am finally loosed and able to stand and walk a few paces to my tent. Ronald is there.

"May I help you?" he asks.

"Thank you, Ronald. Could I have some tea?"

"Yes, I will bring it to you."

I pull off my boots and slide out of my jacket. It is warm again. Then I crawl into my tent and just lie there, not yet asleep, not quite awake. In a few minutes Ronald returns with a cup of hot tea and a plate of scrambled eggs. Room service!

"Nickson said you should eat something," he tells me.

I have not eaten much of anything for four days and have been pushing myself through the most grueling part of the climb. I eat more than half of the eggs, and then fall asleep for the next hour.

When it is time for dinner, I make my way slowly to the mess tent and sit with the group for our evening meal. My appetite is still very weak, but I take some soup and fruit and drink another cup of hot tea. I am now beginning to think it must have been the Diamox that caused the nausea and loss of appetite. The last one I took was two days ago when we left Barafu Camp for the summit. I had intended to take another this morning but forgot to do so. Now, I am starting to feel less nauseated. Being at this lower altitude is probably helping me as well.

At the end of the meal, Nickson steps into the tent for one last briefing about tomorrow. "We will leave about eight o'clock. Our plan is to be at the rendezvous site by noon." Before leaving, Nickson tells us that he and his family are members of a little church outside of Arusha and that they are collecting money for a new building. If we would like to make a contribution, it would be very helpful. He then passes an envelope around the table. As I make a contribution, I think of that old phrase that is often repeated in church circles. "Where two or three are gathered together . . . someone will take an offering."

The campsite is in the thick of the trees, and there are other groups around us. It seems that this area is a major point of departure for folks making the climb and the preferred last campsite for others, such as us. It seems odd to hear voices other than our own after being alone for so long.

I am feeling better as I walk back to the tent. Leo comes by to check on me. "I can't believe we're going to get off this mountain tomorrow," I say to him.

"That'll be great. If you need anything, just yell, my tent is right over there," he tells me.

"Thanks, Leo. Good night."

Journal: *9:18 P.M.*

Oh, it feels so good to be safely back in this tent. What seemed so strange that first night at Forest Camp now seems quite natural. I unzip the top flap of the tent once again in hopes of seeing the stars. However, the trees are so thick above me, I can only catch a glimpse as the branches sway.

What a day. I can't believe we awoke in the crater and now we are here embraced and sheltered by these trees. The wind in the leaves sounds so good. I just have one more day to go. In fact, we should be able to meet the vehicles about noon. I will be home soon!

PRAYER

O Lord, the scripture says that You are our dwelling place. That seems more true to me tonight than ever before. Surely You have been with me, particularly today. Was that You who came to me on the trail? Thank You for Your faithfulness and care. Watch over all of us tonight as we rest. Amen.

14
THE FINAL DAY
SHOWER ANYONE?

*It's when you're safe at home that you wish you were having an adventure.
When you're having an adventure, you wish you were safe at home.*
—Thornton Wilder

Overnight: KLM Flight 571 (37,000 feet)

Journal: *Tuesday, January 31*

*Our final day begins much like every other day on the
mountain—up early, pack up the gear, dress for the day, and
gather in the breakfast tent. Today is the same, but different. We
all know that the end of this grueling experience is nearing. Spirits
are high, yet we try to stay focused and not rush ahead mentally.*

*A few minutes after 8:00, Nickson gives the signal and our
group sets off in a fairly unorganized manner, everyone moving
out at his or her own pace. Our goal is Mweka Gate. It should take
less than four hours. The path passes southwesterly through a tall
stand of scrawny trees and giant heather before dropping fully
into the dense forest. The trail passes along the crest of a narrow
ridge with steep-sided valleys on either side and then broadens to
a wide, well-defined path through the forest.*

*We are surprised to find steps cut into the steeper sections,
and there are channels engraved along much of the path to
prevent erosion. Although the sun is hot, the air remains cool as
we travel under the tall green canopy of the forest. There are dense
tangled patches of forest counterbalanced by sunlit glades where
mosses and lichens glow rich and green in the sun.*

*The path winds back and forth across the forest floor, slipping
over and around obstacles as it descends toward freedom. After*

nearly three hours in the forest, the way becomes a dusty track, which was once a logging trail. About 45 minutes later, the forest opens as we near the end of the trail. At last we emerge amid a bustle of people and Land Rovers at Mweka Gate.

We quickly drop our packs and head for a small building with a well-groomed yard and a large gathering area with restrooms and tables. It is the first outpost of civilization we have seen in over a week. Signing in at the hut, one by one, we begin to find a place to rest. I sit in the shade with Nickson. He tells me he wants to quit climbing, but his options are limited. Work is hard to find in Tanzania, and although climbing is taxing, it also pays well once you become a head guide. He says he is coming to the United States next spring to see some families he met on a previous climb. He hopes to go to New York and California. "Are they far apart?" he asks.

"Yes, there is more than 5,000 kilometers between them." He shakes his head in disbelief. I dig into my pack for a small weatherproof bag. From the bag, I pull a small folder and take one of my business cards and hand it to Nickson saying, "If you get to Chicago, let me know."

"Thank you, John."

Before long, an array of vendors appears from out of nowhere, selling soft drinks and souvenirs. Once everyone has emerged from the forest, we gather at a large outdoor table for a final meal together. At the end of the meal, Nickson announces that it is time for our ceremony. The porters gather around and begin to sing. We scramble for our cameras and recorders. It is a joyful moment.

One by one, porters step forward to dance, and everyone claps and shouts. The trees, the grass, and the flowers join in as well. At the end of the concert, we stand and applaud our companions and friends. Then with the porters still in place, Nickson says in a loud voice, "Certificates."

"First to John, who made it all the way up but had a hard time coming down." I walk forward, shake his hand, and receive a large, official certificate verifying that I had reached Uhuru Peak, the summit of Mount Kilimanjaro. The porters clap once more. Leo, Vince, Tim and Carey, Christian, and Scott all go forward one at a time to the cheers of the group.

Then it is time to go. We bid farewell to the guides and leave Nickson with envelopes of cash to distribute to all who helped on the trip. Four of us—Vince, Scott, Leo, and I—are heading back to Arusha for a shower and a bit of rest before going to the airport to begin our long journey home. Carey, Tim, and Scott are staying on in Tanzania for a few more days to go on safari. The two groups part with hugs, handshakes, and promises to stay in touch.

Once again, our bags are strapped to the top of a Land Rover, as we climb in. What a treat to trade in our weary legs and feet for the comfort of a vehicle. The first part of the drive is on a narrow dirt road through the forest where villages line the road. Before too long we drive out of the trees into the southern slopes of the mountain, which are heavily cultivated. Workers look up from their labor in the fields. Children run to the edge of the road shouting and waving. The dirt track gives way to a paved road.

We drive around the base of the mountain for about 45 minutes and then skirt the edge of Arusha before heading east toward the Kia Lodge, where we had spent our first night. When we arrive about 3:00 in the afternoon, we reclaim the bags we'd left there nine days ago and are given room keys so that we can clean up. Finally!

As soon as I enter the room, I strip off all my clothes, having worn them since Barafu Camp, three days ago. Layer after layer peels away and falls to the floor. With great anticipation, I step carefully into the shower and turn the two handles to start the water. Oh the joy of this moment, I have not bathed in nine days. Turning the handles, I brace myself—but nothing happens. I turn the handles on and off over and over. No water!

I just can't believe it. More than sleep, more than food, more than something cold to drink, I want a shower more than anything. But there is nothing, not a drop. I look at the pile of wet and dirty clothes on the floor. I cannot bear the thought of putting those things back on. I have only one clean set of clothes, which I have saved for the trip home. Those clothes have been in the bag I left at the lodge, but I am still way too dirty to wear them.

What to do?

I notice that I still have two nearly full water bottles in my backpack. It is mountain water, smelling of iodine, but it will have to do. I also remember that there are two bottles of water by the bed, provided by the lodge. So with these four bottles of water, I step back into the shower stall. First the mountain water, I pour about half of one of the bottles slowly over my head and began to soap my face and hair, then a rinse. I repeat this routine, little by little, as I begin to remove one or two layers of topsoil.

After about 15 minutes of careful rationing of my water, I am just barely clean, but not really clean enough to dress or think of making the trip home. I just stand there in the shower for another moment of two, when I hear it—the sound of water starting through the pipes. Can it be? I look up just as the first spray of water from the shower starts—aahh! I stand there for another 10 or 12 minutes and let the water massage my neck and back and arms.

I wash and then wash again. Finally, I am clean, sort of. I dress and begin to organize my things for the return trip. I bury my mountain clothes in the bottom of the rucksack and then add my climbing shoes, gloves, hats, empty bottles, flashlights, and so on. I keep my papers and camera in my backpack that will stay with me throughout the trip home.

Once my things are ready, I walk slowly back to the restaurant area and meet the other guys. We eat an early dinner together. We were exhausted and refreshed at the same time. The meal is very good. This is the first food that has tasted good to me in days. I have only soup and bread, but it is enough. After our meal together, we check in with the staff at the front desk to make arrangements for our trip to the airport.

About 6 P.M., we gather our things and load into the van for the short drive. At the airport we fill out departure forms, pay an exit fee, and present our documents for a final review by the Tanzanian immigration officers. On the other side of this gauntlet is a hot, crowded departure lounge. We find a few seats together and wait.

Surrounding the small lounge area are several airport shops. We take turns watching the bags and walking the perimeter. In one of the nicer shops I notice a beautifully carved Nativity set. I am drawn to it for three reasons. First, it is beautifully done. The wood is high quality, the carving carefully crafted, and the figures look African and natural. Second, Nativity sets are the one thing Jill and I collect. We have 25 or so sets from all around the world. The third and most appealing thing about the set is the small hand-lettered sign set in front of it—"*Activity Set.*"

This misnomer seems right, for surely the birth of Jesus was a supreme example of the activity of God. The Bible puts it like this, "For God so loved the world that he gave his one and only

Son, that whoever believes in him shall not perish but have everlasting life" (John 3:16). I shell out my remaining shillings for the set and a beautiful picture book of Tanzania.

At 9 P.M. our plane arrives, we board and quickly settle in for the short hop from Arusha to Dar es Salaam. Once that stop is complete, we head north for the long flight to Europe.

PRAYER

Dear Heavenly Father,

Thank You for an experience that has reminded me that the things I often view as rights are, in fact, gifts. Thank You for a life of prosperity and opportunity. Why is it that I work in a clean, bright office rather than make my living by carrying heavy loads for others up the mountain? I know that being a president rather than a porter is a gift of grace. O Lord, help me use this gift wisely. May I, in my own way, help others up the mountain. Be with us as we fly tonight. Amen.

15
HOME!

Ah! To do nothing—and do it well.
—Veronique Vienne

Journal: Wednesday, February 1

I wake off and on throughout the night and make myself take a couple of short walks up and down the aisles of the airplane. My legs are stiff and sore. We are served a light breakfast about an hour and a half before starting our descent into Amsterdam.

We land right on time. Once we deplane I check the departure board and determine our respective gates. I am leaving in about three hours for Chicago; Vince is headed to Minnesota, Leo to Boston and then on to Portland, and Scott to Connecticut. We shake hands, thank each other for the friendship and support, then just walk way. What a great group of guys. What an adventure we have shared together.

I stroll through the terminal for nearly an hour. It feels so good to keep moving after the long plane trip. I stop for coffee and a muffin; I am feeling better but am still not up for much food. Then I make my way to a section of the airport where travelers can get day rooms and showers. I make arrangements for a shower. This time there is plenty of hot water! I stand for a long, long time soaking in the experience. Refreshed, I dress and make my way to the gate for the flight home.

I have not slept in a bed for nearly two weeks. Last night was spent on the plane. Now, I will soon be headed home. I can't wait! It has been an amazing trip—all I anticipated and much more. I am sure it will take me a long time to unpack the experience of this climb—my journey has been not only an outward trip of many miles but also an inner journey of attitude and understanding—reflection and release.

I board a KLM Boeing 747, flight 611, at about 10:30 A.M. The flight is smooth. I nap a little, but in reality I am too keyed up to sleep. I am headed home. These hours pass slowly because of my strong sense of anticipation. Finally, we land about eight hours later. It is just after noon, Chicago time. Once I am out of the plane, I turn on my cell phone and when I reach the large waiting area before clearing immigration, I press the speed dial for Jill.

"Hello!" she says.

"It's me . . . and I made it all the way to the top! I am in the immigration line right now, and then I have to get my bag and clear customs. I should be at the curb in about 20 minutes. I can't wait to see you. I will be the guy with the beard."

"I'll be there!"

I am wearing a thin blue windbreaker as I step out of the terminal. Suddenly I am struck by the stiff cold January wind. I had forgotten it was winter. It doesn't matter; I am home. I see Jill's car rounding the corner of the terminal. I start to wave. She flashes her lights and pulls to the curb where I am standing. Hurriedly I load my two bags into the backseat and climb in.

"How was it?" she asks.

"Unbelievable. It was so much more difficult than I ever imagined it would be. And I got sick. I think it was the altitude medicine because I am feeling better now."

We decide to stop on the way home to eat and talk for a while before getting back to campus. Jill calls my office to let the staff know I am back. "The eagle has landed," she says. "He's doing great, and he made it all the way to the summit."

She tells me, "Marjorie [my administrative assistant] says that people have been calling all day to know if she has heard anything."

We drive through downtown Chicago and pull up in front

of one of the city's nicest restaurants for a late lunch. We valet park the car.

"Are your bags OK just sitting in the car like that?" she asks.

"If anyone steals those bags, they are in for a big surprise. There is nothing there but dirty clothes. Who knows, maybe I'll get lucky and someone will take them," I tell her.

We make our way out of the cold Chicago wind and into the restaurant. Jill looks terrific, and I look like a street person on a bad day. I haven't shaved since I left home two weeks ago. I've not been in a bed for the last 10 days. I have hardly eaten for 5 days, but my appetite is now returning.

I order a full meal and we sit alone to talk for the next hour and a half about all I have just been through. Finally, the jet lag kicks in and we head home. I put the seat back and sleep until we pull off the highway, two miles from home.

"Go in the back way," I say to Jill. "I want to see the campus." It is a cold, gray day, but the university looks wonderful. When we pull into the garage and turn off the car, I sit for just a moment, and then whisper, "Thank You, God, for a safe trip."

As I carry my large bag into the house, I say to Jill, "Whatever you do—don't open that bag. I'm serious. I'll take care of it." I take it immediately into the laundry room and load everything into the washer. I sit down for a while and begin to catch up on what had been going on in the real world.

A little later, I call the university chaplain. After visiting for a few moments, I ask if I might have five minutes at the beginning of our campus-wide chapel service the next day to say a quick thank-you to the students for their interest and prayers. After that conversation, I reset the washer for a second wash of the clothes and then I, too, am ready for another shower.

Finally, about 7:30 P.M. I crawl into bed. What a treat—to be home, safe, clean, and in a warm bed. No sleeping bag, no tent, no backpack for a pillow. I think back on my journey with an abiding sense of exhilaration, achievement, and wonder. The journey covered over 16,000 miles, five time zones, and took me from sea level to one of the highest spots on earth.

It is said that Africa is a land of contrasts. It is a continent where the wettest jungles give way to the driest deserts. In a similar way, Kilimanjaro is a mountain of contrasts as well. I think back on the lush forest and the harsh crater floor. I remember hot sun and freezing wind where peaks and valleys coexist in a tranquil tension. The mountain is life itself: good and bad, exhilarating and discouraging, sunshine and shadow, peaceful and dangerous, all at once.

Life is a journey—filled with mountains.

PRAYER

O dear God, I am home! I am home. Thank You again for Your faithful care and keeping. May I never take such gifts for granted. I pray tonight for Ronald, whose kindness brightened my way. I pray for Nickson, Freddie, and Joachim who labor hard for their daily bread. And be with my friends from the mountain. I may never see their faces again, but I shall not forget the joy of their company. Bless Leo, Vince, Scott, Christian, Tim, and Carey. Amen.

THE PRINCIPLE OF PERSPECTIVE

*The ability to see and grasp all of the relevant data
in a meaningful relationship.*

———————

Things look differently once you have stood on the
top of the mountain. Having done the difficult thing,
all other things seem less menacing. Life is hard, so what?

16

TRAVELING LIGHT

Casting all your care upon Him, for He cares for you.
I Pet. 5:7, NKJV

One of the challenges of getting ready for the Kilimanjaro climb was to make sure I was packing enough, but not too much. As I look back on the trip, I think my careful preparation and anticipation paid off. I carried what I needed, but not much more. When I unpacked at the end of the trip, there was only one shirt I had not worn, which was tucked away in the bottom of my bag.

The climb underscored how taxing it would have been to make that journey carrying more than I needed; and yet how many times do people trudge through life with burdens, cares, concerns, and responsibilities that not only weigh them down and impede their progress but also sap the joy from the journey. There is genuine value in traveling light as we journey through life.

Each year, the city of Chicago selects a Book of the Year as a way to foster literary thought and discussion throughout the city. The book is read in the public schools, talked about in the cultural circles of the area, promoted in several ways, and critiqued at the city's colleges and universities.

The book selected a couple of years ago was *The Things They Carried,* by award-winning writer Tim O'Brien. The book is a collection of interrelated stories and essays set in the midst of the Vietnam War. In the first chapter, O'Brien introduces the reader to a cast of characters who reappear throughout the rest of the book. He introduces them by describing "the things they carried" during the war.

O'Brien tells the story of a young first lieutenant named Jimmy Cross who carried with him a set of letters from a girl back home. "They were not love letters, but Lieutenant Cross was hoping." He kept the letters wrapped in plastic, and in the late afternoon "he would dig his foxhole, wash his hands under a canteen," and carefully unwrap his treasure. Holding those notes "with the tips of his fingers" he would spend the last few moments of daylight pretending.

The book also describes a native American soldier, a devout Baptist, who carried a new Testament with him. This was a gift from his father who taught Sunday School each week in Oklahoma City. "As a hedge against bad times," he also carried with him "his grandmother's distrust of the white man and his grandfather's old hunting hatchet."

They carried all the emotional baggage of men who might die. Grief, terror, love, longing—these were intangibles, but the intangibles had their own mass and specific gravity, they had tangible weight. They carried their own lives. The pressures were enormous. They shared the weight of memory. They took up what others could no longer bear. By and large, they carried these things inside, maintaining the masks of composure. And often they carried each other, the wounded or weak.[17]

Tim O'Brien's image of a person carrying various items as he or she moves through the demands of life and death is a metaphor I'd thought about as I sat alone in a dimly lit tent on the other side of the world.

For 35 years, I have watched people come and go from the campus where I've lived and worked as a student, professor, pastor, and president. I see freshmen arrive at the university each fall; seniors leave each spring, and alumni and friends, representing different years, different decades, and different stages of life, come and go as well. And I also look at my own life across this same time.

In the O'Brien book, the individuals were defined by what they carried . . . and so are we. A freshman arrives carrying hopes and dreams and aspirations, but he or she also carries a measure of anxiety packed into some corner of a suitcase or a book bag. Seniors leave carrying with them plenty of memories and lots of lessons learned (some of them in class). They carry a new set of hopes and dreams and some new angst as well.

We are all defined, to some degree, by what we carry, what we refuse to carry, and what we cast away. The choice to carry something or to lay it aside is a decision we make with many of the things we pick up over time.

And we certainly do pick up things along the way. We pick up responsibilities, influence, and authority. We carry added financial pressures and sometimes a health issue. Over time we gain relationships, successes, and failures. We carry memories, scars, and lots of incidental cares and worries.

Sometimes our hopes and dreams are replaced with disappointment, even disillusionment, and suddenly (yet not so suddenly), we find we are burdened down by "the things we carry."

Peter knew about this business of carrying. He had run the full gamut of ups and downs in his life and in his walk with Jesus, so in writing to the Early Church (and to you and me) he says, "Cast all your anxiety on him because he cares for you" (1 Pet. 5:7).

The Living Bible (TLB) reads, "Let him have all your worries and cares, for he is always thinking about you and watching everything that concerns you." In *The Message* (TM) it is, "Live carefree before God; he is most careful with you."

There is an interesting clustering of words in these translations—*care, cares, carry, careful,* and *carefree*. Christ desires to carry our cares, for He cares for us. "Come to Me, all you who labor and are heavy laden, and I will give you rest" (Matt. 11:28, NKJV).

The verse in 1 Peter is a declaration, a promise, and an invitation all in one single sentence. It is an echo of Ps. 55:22 that says, "Cast your cares on the LORD and he will sustain you." It brings to mind the beautiful passage from Isaiah that says, "He has borne our griefs and carried our sorrows" (53:4, NKJV).

Will there be problems? Yes. We only have to read 1 Peter to know how true that is. In chapter 1 it says, "Now for a little while you may have had to suffer grief in all kinds of trials" (v. 6). In chapter 4 Peter writes, "Dear friends, do not be surprised at the painful trial you are suffering, as though something strange were happening to you" (v. 12).

To be alive is to confront challenges, difficulties, obstacles, and the cares and anxieties that come with them. The question is not how to avoid the cares of life; the issue is what to do with those cares. We are not to be defined by our anxiety. If, using O'Brien's idea, people know us by the things we carry, then let us not be defined by our anxiety but rather by our faith.

We cannot control all of the things that may come our way. And I know that when troubles come, we cannot simply ignore them. But what we can do is lay aside the anxiety, which robs us of our peace. Anxiety tends to distract and divide our mind and heart so that we fall short of fully trusting God. Thus Peter says, "Cast all your anxiety on him."

Cares are cast on Him by the power of our faith, by believing that His grace and goodness will sustain us and that God will indeed work in all things for our good. Remember the words of Jesus in the Sermon on the Mount: "Therefore I tell you, do not worry about your life, what you will eat or drink; or about your body, what you will wear. Is not life more important than food, and the body more important than clothes? Look at the birds of the air; they do not sow or reap or store away in barns, and yet your heavenly Father feeds them. Are you not much more valuable than they?" (Matt. 6:25-26). The choice we must make is whether to let go of anxiety and take hold of faith, knowing that He cares for us.

What a wonderful affirmation this is. And think once more about who it is that is writing. It is Peter, impulsive Peter, who was rebuked by Jesus, who denied Him; and yet it is Peter to whom Jesus reached out with special care following the Resurrection.

We have a choice to carry our cares or to cast our cares upon the One who cares for us. In his book *Lion and Lamb: The Relentless Tenderness of Jesus*, Brennan Manning tells the story of a man dying of cancer.[18] His wife is already gone. He is living now with his only daughter and her family. She, naturally, is worried about him. When a new priest arrives at her church, she implores him to come visit her father.

So, a couple of days later, the priest stops by, unannounced. He greets the family and then makes his way to the back bedroom to introduce himself to the old man. He knocks gently and the man says, "Come in."

"Hello, Joseph," says the priest. "I just stopped by to meet you and to visit for a few minutes. Is that all right?"

"Sure, Father," the man says. "Please come in."

As the priest steps fully into the room, he notices a chair has been pulled up close to the bed. "Are you expecting someone?" he asks.

"Oh, the chair. Would you mind closing the door?"

Puzzled, the priest quietly shuts the door.

"I have never told anyone this, not even my daughter," says the man, "but all my life I have never known how to pray . . . until one day about four years ago when my best friend said to me, 'Joe, prayer is just a simple matter of having a conversation with Jesus. Here's what I suggest: sit down on a chair and place an empty chair in front of you and in faith, see Jesus on the chair. He's promised, "I'll be with you always." Then just speak to Him and listen in the same way you're doing with me right now.'

"So, Father, I tried it and I liked it so much that I do it often, especially these days. I'm careful, though. If my daughter saw me talking to an empty chair she would really worry."

Following his visit, the priest asked the daughter to call him in a day or so to let him know how her father was getting along. Two days later, she called to tell the priest that her father had died.

"Did he seem to die in peace?" asked the priest.

"Yes," she said. "But there was something odd, Father. Apparently, just before Daddy died, he leaned over and rested his head on a chair beside his bed."

Peter said, "Cast all your anxiety on him because he cares for you."

Maybe the writer Tim O'Brien got it wrong after all. Perhaps we are not defined by the things we carry but rather by the One who carries us.

17

A CONVERSATION AT 35,000 FEET

Therefore go and make disciples of all nations ...
—Jesus (Matt. 28:19)

This trip to Kilimanjaro brought to mind a conversation I had on my first flight back from Africa 20 years ago. It was early on a Saturday morning, and I was hustling to make it back from a mission trip to Kenya. I had been there for about three weeks, working, speaking, traveling, and meeting people from early morning until late at night.

I'd left Nairobi at midnight the night before and had flown till dawn to reach Amsterdam where I slept for a couple of hours in a rather uncomfortable chair in the departure lounge of the airport until my next flight was ready. As I boarded the plane, I was still tired. I found the right row and slid into my seat—hoping to sleep my way to the United States. I grabbed a flight pillow, leaned my head back, closed my eyes, and took a deep breath. In a moment I felt the seat jar and turned to my right to see a man just settling in beside me. I nodded but didn't smile and I didn't speak. I thought to myself, why are these planes always so crowded? Thankfully he appeared to be the quiet type.

The flight service attendants finished their preflight routine as we were being pushed gently away from the gate. We taxied for a moment or two and then paused for a long time-out on the tarmac. As we sat there waiting for our final clearance to depart, I closed my eyes again. Just as I was starting to drift off to sleep, those great engines came to life with a roar unmatched by any lion I'd heard out on the Serengeti. Suddenly we were speeding down the runway at full throttle, lifting off and beginning our westward race with the sun.

I resettled back into my seat and closed my eyes once more when the man beside me asked, "Where have you been?"

"I am returning home from a visit to Nairobi, Kenya, in East Africa," I replied.

"Vacation?"

"No, I went for a couple of weeks to help some missionaries there."

"Huh," the fellow said. "I can't believe there are still missionaries in the world. You don't hear much about them anymore."

He looked prosperous. I would say he was slightly older than me. I responded, "That's true, I suppose, but there are still a lot of missionaries in the world."

"Well, I don't get it," he said, shaking his head as if to say, Isn't that strange that people still go to be missionaries? How quaint.

So I turned a little bit more in his direction and said, "If a person goes abroad to study, we think he or she is bright and gifted. If an individual works abroad, we think of him or her as wealthy and industrious. If a person travels abroad for extended periods, we think of that person as privileged and cultured. If someone serves his or her country abroad in the army or in the diplomatic service, we see that individual as patriotic.

"If a person lives abroad as part of the Peace Corps, we consider him or her a humanitarian. But isn't it strange," I continued, "that if a person lives, works, travels, studies, and serves abroad as a missionary, folks see that as fanatical or at least . . . odd?"

"Well," he said, "we used to have missionaries at my church

a long time ago, and they always seemed to be kind of strange."

"Well, they start out as ordinary people," I replied. "Then they get a vision and a calling that takes them halfway around the world, where they live and work for years at a time. When they do come home, they may not know anything about pro sports or the latest scandal in Hollywood or Washington. Their clothes, at first, might be even a bit out of style.

"Some have been gone long enough that they have had dysentery and have had to help others through malaria. In the time they have been overseas, some have seen people die needlessly. They have missed their own families and have learned of a parent's passing after the fact. They have sent their children to a distant city for boarding school.

"So we should not think it odd if they may seem a little awkward upon reentry into western culture. On the other hand, if you could stand with them in the marketplace in Nairobi or Quito or Hong Kong or Calcutta or wherever, you would be amazed at their fluency and the ease of their conversation."

"Well, maybe so," he said. "But it just seems that they are a bit fanatical."

"That depends on one's point of view," I replied. "Tomorrow, all across the United States, there will be stadiums filled with loud and passionate fans; some will paint their faces and wear bright-colored shirts with big numbers. They will scream and shout and wave their arms as they cheer for one team or the other. We see that as normal. But how is it that for a person to have the same level of passion for God and for other people, when they want to care for the sick and feed the hungry and comfort the dying and teach the poor, and when they do it all for no money but in the name of Jesus, we think it's strange?

"I heard of a missionary in the Far East who had been there for many years when one of America's great companies came to offer him a job, since he knew the language and the customs and he had connections. The missionary listened politely then said, 'No, thank you.' In response the company upped their offer, but he said, 'No, really, I'm not interested.' They offered him more money. Finally he said to them, 'It's not that your salary is too small, it's that the job is too small. I am doing something so much more important.'

"It is similar to the time some folks were visiting with Mother Teresa in India while she was caring for a dying woman who was very ill. One visitor had to turn his head. Later he said to her, 'Mother, I wouldn't do that for a million dollars.'

"'Neither would I,' replied Mother Teresa.

"They don't do it for the money," I said to the man in the seat beside me.

The flight attendant came by, he took a Diet Coke, and I had tomato juice. And we both were handed roasted peanuts in the little packet. As I was struggling, trying to open mine with my teeth, he asked, "Are you a preacher?"

"Yes."

"Do you mind if I talk to you for a few minutes?"

"I don't mind."

His face registers a look as though he has decided to go deeper into all of this and perhaps even to take me on a bit.

"I think what turns me off," he said, "is that I believe others have as much right to their religion as we have to ours. I mean, where do we get off trying to change them?"

"Live and let live, is that what you mean?" I asked.

He nodded.

"I know that philosophy seems to be correct, and we are living in an age where there is great tolerance for tolerance," I said. "But I don't think that view is right."

"Sure it is," he said.

didn't let members of certain Mormon sects have as
s they wanted to have," I countered. "Courts over-
ho withhold medical attention from their children
even when it is done on religious grounds. And if some religious
group in the United States said they believed in cannibalism, you
can be sure we'd put a stop to it. And we all abhor the violence
that takes place, from time to time, in the name of religion.

"The problem," I continued, "is that this idea that all religions ought to be able to practice as freely as they want rests on
the assumption that all religions have equal value. And I for one
don't believe that.

"I know there is the myth that the unreached peoples of the
world live in a kind of bliss of ignorance and that they are happy
and fulfilled in their animism or superstition or ancestor wor-
ship, or whatever, and we should simply leave them alone.

"But that is just a myth. It is in these cultures where the witness and word of Christ is absent that evil often reigns
unchecked. And by the way, if you want to say that all religions
are of equal worth, then you would have to include the religion
of the missionaries we're talking about. And if every religion
can do what it wants, then these missionaries are well within
their rights. You want to be tolerant of everything—but them.

"The fact is, we ought to oppose things that harm people.
We can't go on the assumption that all religions are true, for the
simple reason that religions do not agree. Something cannot be
true and untrue at the same time. If one religion says that there
is one God and another religion says there are many gods, they
both can't be true.

"Truth by its very nature is narrow and intolerant. I mean,
two plus two doesn't make five, no matter how sincere you are.
There are things that are true and things that are false.

"Missionaries go believing and teaching that Jesus Christ is the truth. They don't go out to proclaim democracy or capitalism or technology or even denominationalism. They go because they believe in Jesus Christ and they believe the Bible. Jesus said, for example, 'I am the way and the truth and the life. No man comes to the Father but by me.'

"Jesus is not saying that we are to simply embrace a code of conduct or a set of philosophical assumptions. He is declaring, 'I am the truth.' Thus He calls us to a spiritual relationship.

"He claims to be Lord, and once a person finds Him to be Lord, the response we make is one of service and obedience to God and to others in His name. This Jesus commands His followers to 'Go into all the world and make disciples.' Christian missionaries and the churches that support them are simply responding to the clear call of God in Christ, for this world belongs completely to God."

Suddenly there was turbulence; the plane began to bounce up and down. It was as if I had orchestrated some special effect to underscore the power of God.

"Well," he said as he began to reenter the conversation, "when you change a man's religion, you change his culture and you destroy who he is. What right do we have to change another person's culture? That is elitist, isn't it?" he asked.

"Do you really believe that?" I asked.

"Sure," he nodded.

So I said, "Do you really think it is wrong to change and influence another person's culture? If you believe that, you have to be consistent. You can't speak of it just in religious terms. If you really believe that it is wrong to influence another's person's culture and, if you are going to be consistent, then you are not going to go into the American ghetto near you and try to change the culture of that drug pusher or prostitute.

"Live and let live, remember?

"And you are not going to go to the racist culture of the Ku Klux Klan to try to influence those people to put away their hatred and bigotry.

"I mean, if you really believe that it is wrong to influence other cultures, then you will not teach the ignorant and you will not seek to bring hygiene to communities where disease is rampant. I think it is, in fact, an act of immorality not to try to change some ways of living that are harmful and degrading. Not all cultures are equally good; some are dehumanizing.

"And what about the presence of American business interests in foreign countries? The presence of American business and military has done more to impact foreign culture than missionaries. And many of those alterations are suspect, to say the least.

"Missionaries are generally quite culturally sensitive. They take the time to learn the language and live with the people, not in isolation from them on bases and business compounds. American businesses have 150 people overseas for every one missionary there.

"The church seeks to change culture that is destructive, but under other circumstances the church seeks to be culturally sensitive and to respect the good that is there."

The flight attendant came by and served our meals . . .

He began again, "All I am trying to say is that here we are, America, a Christian county, and we have murder, rape, racism, and this huge drug problem. If we have no more to show for our Christianity than we do, how do we get by telling others how to live?"

"First of all," I replied, "it sounds very humble to say that we should not try to make anyone else better until we solve all of our own problems. But I must challenge you again to be consistent. If you adopt that philosophy, then that means we must close our schools, because our teachers and administrators are not perfect. And that means we must also close our hospitals because our hospitals, our doctors and nurses and technicians, are not perfect.

"If you're going to demand that our house be perfectly in order before we reach out to others, nothing will ever be done.

"Certainly American society, as well as the church, is less than it ought to be. Nonetheless, the church has the highest standards and the worthiest goals in all the world. While it may not always meet those goals and standards, the church has done more good for more people around the world than any other agency in all of the history of the world."

We were quiet for a long while. Then the great airship began its final descent. In a few moments we were touching down. The tires screeched, the engines cried out, and the plane shook as if it did not want to be tethered to the earth again.

As we stood to leave, gathering our things, I said, "Is Chicago your final destination?"

"No, I'm going on," he said.

We shake hands; I walk down the aisle and wonder to myself if I have said the right things, in the right way, at the right time. When I got inside the terminal, I stopped for a moment and looked across the way at the man. I thought about his last words to me.

He said, "I'm going on." Those words echoed in my mind. "I'm going on." Where, I wondered? For all his accomplishments and all his intellect, he didn't seem to have a clear sense of direction in his life. He was widely traveled, but it seemed to me that he traveled aimlessly, swept along, not by conviction or purpose, but with the varied tides of time and culture.

I will say this for him, however. He was a good teacher. He taught me that one does not have to go to Africa to be a missionary or find a mission field. People all around us need to know of God's love and His power; sometimes it's the person seated right there at your elbow.

Jesus said, "All authority in heaven and on earth has been given to me. Therefore go and make disciples . . . And surely I am with you always, to the very end of the age" (Matt. 28:18-20).

18
SOLITUDE

Solitude is the school of genius.
—Edward Gibbon

One of the lessons of the mountain was the value of extended periods of solitude. Although I was with a small group of people; most of my time was spent alone. There were occasions of social interaction, discussion, and laughter, as well as serious conversation among the group. However, day after day, particularly as the trip wore on and the elevations and demands of the climb increased, walking was done in silence, because breathing was difficult and talking was taxing.

Meals were communal; but during the most challenging stretch of the trip, we often ate in relative silence, being both weary from the journey and anxious about the demands still looming before us. Following our evening meal, we would crawl into our tents and spend each night alone. In my small tent during those hours, the world outside, with all of its dangers and demands, was shut out and the world within (my thoughts and emotions) was shut in.

The ascent of Mount Kilimanjaro provided an extended time away from the routines and demands of my normal days. This was refreshing for me. My job is people-intensive. I love it; but to constantly give to others creates a need to replenish the spirit, calm the inner person, and reflect carefully on the nature of one's life. Being too busy and too much with others can create a kind of "living in the third person," where taking one's cues and making judgments is too easily surrendered to the crowd.

Solitude is an escape; but it is not running away or refusing to face the demands of life. In fact, when well used, times alone serve to renew and refresh and thus equip us to more effectively cope with the pressures of daily life. Raymon Inmon said, "If you are seeking creative ideas, go out walking. Angels whisper to a man when he goes for a walk."[19]

The only time a person can truly call his or her own is that which he or she has privately. The rest belongs to others; it is shared time, invested time, time spent. To balance life, in the midst of living on the time and schedule of others, individuals need to plan for and preserve moments of solitude and peace. My father used to call it "lookin' out the window time." As a boy I never knew what he was talking about. Now I find myself longing for such moments.

The ability to be alone is valuable. In a culture where interpersonal relationships and/or simply being with people is often considered the answer to almost any form of distress, it is sometimes difficult to think that solitude can be as therapeutic as emotional support. Solitude promotes insight, and insight can foster a deeper sense of well-being.

It seems to me that after periods of solitude, a person's presence and contributions to society can be more authentic. Often I experience a deepening of my own self-understanding, the seeds of which were initially garnered from interaction with others, but only fully realized in times alone.

The Bible has much to say about the benefits and blessings that come from taking time to be alone with God. "In quietness and trust is your strength," the prophet Isaiah wrote (Isa. 30:15). The psalmist delivers this message, "Be still, and know that I am God" (Ps. 46:10). The Jewish understanding of Sabbath carries with it some sense of this need for solitude. The Sabbath is for rest.

Repeatedly, the Gospel writers noted how often Jesus would withdraw from the crowd and even from His closest followers. His public ministry was preceded by 40 days of solitude in the wilderness. The Lord would often go up to a high place or onto the lake to be alone. Even at the moment of His greatest struggle, He left His disciples and went on alone a little further into the depths of the Garden of Gethsemane.

Across the ages, Christian tradition has reinforced the values of solitude. Religious communities and orders were formed and sustained for centuries to provide silence and spiritual blessings accrued through prayer, meditation, and service. Monasteries and convents are places where men and women go to practice the monastic life, to live the quiet life of contemplation, prayer, simplicity, and work. These are communities; yet they are communities built on solitude.

Obviously, the monastic life in a formal sense is not meant for many. Yet "'tis not the habit that makes the monk." So it is possible that the lessons and benefits of such a reflective life can be experienced, at least in part, by individuals who live in the larger world amid a matrix of relationships, families, careers, and friends. By taking some time for quiet reflection each day, it is feasible to bring part of the monastic life into our busy routines and crowded lives and, by so doing, deepen the quality and texture of every other aspect of life.

Twenty-first-century life has created a pace and view of life that erodes both the time available for solitude and personal comfort with being alone. Everything seems to shout, "Look at me; listen to me. Now!" Such an environment conditions us to think we always need to be reading, watching, or listening.

Often, I have come home to an empty house and immediately turned on the television or radio. It is not that I am particularly interested in whatever happens to be on. I am just conditioned to noise. Think how frequently you see individuals out for a walk or a run, only to notice the earphones from their I-pods or cell phones.

And interestingly this need for noise lingers even when we are silent. In our attempts to be still, often our internal chatter goes on and on. Perhaps it is this inner dialogue, this ever-present self-talk, that we seek to silence by turning up the volume around us.

The climb of Mount Kilimanjaro delivered me from clutter and forced me to be alone. This type of isolation was not for rest or relaxation, nor for fun. Those moments can bring blessing and restoration; but there are other kinds of solitude as well. My quiet retreat was packed with challenge, anxiety, frustration, and fatigue. These, I learned, can also be avenues of blessings.

Being submerged in nature also added to the benefits of my time away, for nature is indeed a good therapist. The wind in my face, the sun on my back, and the feel of the rocks all communicated a sense of proportion and place as I thought about life, my life and my role in the world. Environment educates.

Walking is treading upon the earth, on God's creation, but it is more than that. Doing so reminds us of our humanity, our place. Like the liturgy of Ash Wednesday, the natural world prompts us saying, "Remember that thou art dust, and unto dust thou shall return" (see Gen. 3:19).

How beneficial it can be for any of us to simply take a walk, work in the yard, or stroll on the shore. It is in these times of being alone that we encounter ourselves in new and often deeper ways. There is pleasure in solitude. Kierkegaard said that most people pursue pleasure with such breathless haste they hurry past it.

How often have I failed to slow down, even a little, to enjoy the moment? When I am pressed, I eat too fast, hardly taking enough time to enjoy my meal. I am like a racer pulling into the pit—tires are changed, windows washed, and fuel added in 12 seconds, then back into the race.

A few years ago I stayed in a home where the family pet was a little white rat named Crackers. It lived in a cage beside the kitchen table. As I came downstairs early the first morning for a solitary cup of coffee, I realized I was under surveillance. I was being watched from three feet away by a pair of tiny red eyes.

Throughout the weekend, Crackers would climb onto a wheel inside the cage and run and run. Perhaps, for the pet, such an activity was a harmless, maybe even helpful, diversion. For people, however, such a rat race, a treadmill with no end and no goal, extracts a terrific toll. It wears us physically, emotionally, and spiritually.

There are three types of people who are most likely to get trapped in a rat race existence. First is the individual who has a driving need to be successful or a passion for achievement. Second is the overcommitted individual, the person who cannot say no. And third is the person who must always live up to an unrealistic self-expectation of perfection or to the desires of others.

There is a word from God concerning the rat race routine. In Isaiah's 40th chapter, one of the silver chapters in a golden book, are these words of encouragement:

Do you not know? Have you not heard? The LORD is the everlasting God, the Creator of the ends of the earth. He will not grow tired or weary, and his understanding no one can fathom. He gives strength to the weary and increases the power of the weak. Even youths grow tired and weary, and young men stumble and fall; but those who hope in the LORD will renew their strength. They will soar on wings like eagles; they will run and not grow weary, they will walk and not be faint *(vv. 28-31)*.

The verse immediately preceding this passage is almost modern in the despondency it reveals. The complaint is this: "My way is hidden from the LORD; my cause is disregarded by my God" (v. 27). In response, the prophet offers two questions that focus not on the human situation but upon the divine adequacy. One of the questions deals with the present, "Do you not know?" The other is cast in the past tense, "Have you not heard?"

What is it that we should know? What have we heard, yet not remembered?

• God's Eternal Nature—"The LORD is the everlasting God." For those of us who feverishly look at our watches, diligently study our calendars, and become enslaved by our schedules, Isaiah says—don't forget to look to the eternal one—"The LORD is the everlasting God, the Creator of the ends of the earth." There is only One who stands beyond it all, and the Bible calls us to stop our frantic run from place to place to place—stop and remember God's eternal nature.

• The Inexhaustibility of God's Resources—"He will not grow tired or weary."

There are four stages of the human rat race. First, there is a task or a challenge. With this comes a sense of excitement and the anticipation of achievement. The second stage is commitment; the decision to pursue the goal. After a time, however, the pursuit becomes routine and perfunctory and leads to the third stage of the rat race, which is containment. We are trapped and driven by what we once pursued with energy and joy. Fourth is collapse. We quit caring. We burn out. We quit. It is a moment of implosion and exhaustion of body, mind, and spirit. Too many folks experience this pattern: challenge, commitment, containment, and sometimes collapse.

In contrast to this cycle, the Bible says, "Those who hope in the LORD will renew their strength. They will soar on wings like eagles; they will run and not grow weary, they will walk and not be faint." What a change—from rat race to eagle's wings.

When an eagle is soaring, it is flying, not by its own power, but by the great unseen thermal currents rising from the earth. The eagle soars on the strength of the wind, and so may we. The breath of God, His Holy Spirit, can so fill a person's life with His presence that there results a buoyancy and lift of spirit that enables any who puts their hope in the Lord to rise above the rat race.

Why run when you can soar!

Many successful climbers of the corporate ladder recognize too late that they were so earnest, so hardworking, so intent to go higher and higher that they missed a vital element in their pursuit: the ladder was leaning against the wrong wall. It is only when they arrive at the top that it hits them. How often do people succeed at work only to fail in life? Solitude provides moments along the way to evaluate and remember it is never too late to find a new wall or climb a different ladder.

One of the favorite phrases of the church father Jerome was *"solvitur ambulando,"* which means "It is solved walking." In other words, if you have a crisis to face, a problem to understand, a decision to make, or a difficult question to resolve— take a hike!

Jerome is perhaps best known for translating the entire Bible from its original languages into Latin. Throughout this long and tedious process, he would regularly leave his writing table to walk, returning a few minutes later to translate a stubborn sentence into smooth-flowing language, the hallmark of his translation.

Walking solves problems because it allows the inner person to rest and reflect while the outer person works. Such an activity refreshes the intellect and spirit. What a bargain. It is an enjoyable, healthy, and refreshing way to solve problems, and it's free! Perhaps the fourth-century challenges and problems faced by Jerome are not much different from ours.

The capacity to be alone is a valuable resource, which facilitates learning, thinking, innovation, and coming to terms with change. It fosters contact with the inner world of imagination and wonder. By being alone, an individual can pray, reflect, and develop a personal relationship with God that cannot be attained through any other avenue.

> *When from our better selves we have too long*
> *Been parted by the hurrying world, and droop,*
> *Sick of its business, of its pleasures tired,*
> *How gracious, how benign, is Solitude.*[20]

Although men and women are social beings who certainly need interaction with others, they also need time alone. We need reflection as well as relationships. It's all about balance and equilibrium—body, mind, and spirit. Time away, even for brief periods, can significantly help bring about coherence.

When a person withdraws for time alone, particularly time alone with God, interior balance is restored. He or she is *re-centered* in contrast to being *ec-centric*, or out of center. The philosopher John Locke made an interesting point when he observed, "The thoughts that often come unsought, and, as it were, drop into the mind, are commonly the most valuable of any we have."

As I climbed the mountain day after day and spent nights in solitude, I found this statement of Locke's to be true. Thoughts came once my pace had slowed. Things I had been wrestling to understand seemed clearer as I turned the volume down and spent time alone.

I also developed a keener sense of God. I experienced what Brother Lawrence meant when he spoke of "practicing the presence" of God. God was all around me. Nature was the canvas and the megaphone. But this deeper sense of God was more than the wonder of nature, it was an inner presence as well—a still, small voice that could be heard more clearly once I was quiet.

Not long ago, I was reminded of a saying from the famous baseball player Satchel Paige. Not only was he a fine ball player, but he also understood life. He was full of wisdom and joy. On one occasion when talking with the press about how he prepared himself mentally to pitch in a big game he said, "Sometimes I sits and thinks, and sometimes I just sits." His comments remind us that our quiet time, our moments of stillness, need not be structured. Sometimes it is helpful to read a devotional passage or to focus on a particular problem of concern, but other times it may be just as valuable to "just sit."

David Kundtz suggests that America should have an annual National Stopping Day, a one-day retreat. He writes:

Everyone would be quiet and listen. The preachers. The politicians. The judges. The lawyers. The journalists. There'd be nothing on television or radio. No newspapers. No mail delivered. Only necessary phone calls. The World Wide Web would be still.

All over the country we could look at the sky, take a walk, watch the rain, listen to nature, sit quietly, look into one another's eyes, say a few good words, walk the dog, eat quietly, and observe the passage of time.

Just imagine how we would all feel the day after! I've no doubt we'd all demand that it become a monthly event.[21]

My climb taught me the blessings of solitude, to be still and know God. It is in silence and solitude that the external and internal noises of life fade and God communicates His will and His way.

19

STRANGERS AND FRIENDS

"E Pluribus Unum"

One of the main things I looked forward to as I planned my African adventure was to experience the interpersonal dynamic of meeting a group of strangers one day and setting off together the very next day to do one of the most difficult things on earth. It was not just the climb I anticipated; it was the climb together from which I hoped to learn much.

Spending those days with Tim and Carey, Scott, Christian, Vince, and Leo was a vital part of the trip. Their constant presence, stretching out in a line before me on the trail or walking by my side, made each day's journey better. We were strangers at first; but little by little, out of many we become one.

What does it take for a group of individuals to become a team capable of conquering a great mountain? Can those characteristics be fostered within a family, a congregation, or a group at work?

First, it takes *authenticity*. Because I am a university president and live on campus in the midst of a small town, I am recognized almost everywhere I go. When I walk across campus, enter a restaurant or a place of business in town, or attend a public meeting, I am not John; I am the president. Being defined by my role does not automatically make me less authentic, but it does drape my personality and persona with a robe of expectations that colors both how I am perceived by others and how I see myself. In such a situation, an individual must be careful to not simply become a public person who over time loses touch with his or her inner authentic self.

A public person needs a clear sense of self that rests not on the profession he or she occupies but flows from an inner core of self-awareness and character. I should not, must not, be one person as the president of the university and another when I am alone or where no one knows me. The Kilimanjaro experience stripped my outer identity of those things that reside alone in the office I hold.

When I walked to the breakfast table at Kia Lodge my first morning in Africa, I was not a university president or a minister or Dr. Bowling. I was John, a somewhat crazy nonclimber who thought he could do this thing. My companions on the journey did not see me through the lens of office or role; they saw me as just another climber.

In reality, no one on the trip cared too much about what I did professionally. They cared about who I was and if I was an authentic person—not an individual playing a role or living out a set of exterior expectations. It is a good thing to occasionally step out of our official formal roles, those things we do professionally that define us, and out of our comfort zones to find ourselves once more.

Oscar Wilde, the playwright, once suggested that most people are other people. By that he meant their thoughts are someone else's thoughts, their views the view of the crowd, their lives a mimicry, and their words mere quotations. Although Wilde had a cynical streak, he was perhaps correct in observing how easy it is to live our lives in the third person, rather than discovering and nurturing our true selves. "One's real life is often the life that one does not lead," he wrote.

Someone has suggested that misfortune does not change people; it unmasks them. The same could be said about meeting a challenge in life. In the taxing moments when we must climb the mountain, our true self is revealed. "It's no use walking anywhere to preach unless our walking is our preaching," observed Francis of Assisi. Authenticity is important for team building.

Second, if a group is going to hold together across difficult days, there must be a measure of *consideration*. Almost from the first moment, without ever stating it, there was an understanding that the trip was not about any one of us; it was about all of us. I think it was Tim who stated it first with a strong sense of conviction, "We're all going to make it to the top. Let's just decide that right now. We can do it together."

The 21st-century world we live in fosters a "me first" mentality. The arrows of culture and media have a way of turning inward. But if a group of individuals at work or at home is to be at its best, each person needs to see his or her role and identity not in isolation but in relationship to others.

There are two ways of spreading light: be the candle or the mirror that reflects it. Consideration focuses on the light from others. It is an interesting irony that we must work at being reminded that the entire population of the universe, with one exception, is composed of others. Life is not about me; it is about us.

What is my role as part of this team? How can I help bring out the best in others? How can I help my colleagues or family members be successful? Those are the questions that reverse the flow of an inwardly focused society and help foster community.

Third, this spirit of consideration, once properly understood, expresses itself in *encouragement*. It may have been Christian, more than any other member of our group, who always seemed to have a positive word. The trip was not easy for him, or any of us, yet as we walked or rested or gathered for our meals, Christian seemed to say the right things to the right persons to keep our spirits up. He looked for ways to encourage us individually. His conversation was focused, not on himself, but always on someone else. Because of this characteristic of Christian, as we struggled our way up the mountain, when we paused for a break, or when we ate our meals together, all of us wanted to have at least a brief conversation with him. He was an encourager.

Having someone speak a word of encouragement to you, to bless you with his or her confidence and concern, is like taking a cool drink of water when you are parched. It refreshes your whole being. Mark Twain once commented that he could live a month on a good compliment. We all need to be noticed and valued and spoken to with genuine interest and respect.

A fourth element of teamwork is *patience.* Anybody married? Marriage is the most elemental partnership; and one of the graces that make a marriage successful is the simple virtue of patience. The same is true on the mountain, on the job, or in the church. We stay together, patiently.

Humility is another part of the team-building equation. Years ago, when I was a boy and the New York Yankees had won yet another World Series, which they seemed to do every year during that era, a reporter was interviewing a player named Lefty Gomez, a star pitcher for the Yankees. The reporter asked this question, "Lefty, what is the secret of your success?"

"Clean livin' and a fast outfield," he replied. What he was saying was this: Even when I give it my very best effort; when I throw my finest pitch, even then, on occasion, someone will hit the ball over my head and beyond my reach. When that happens, my success, my win/loss record, is in the hands of my teammates. Someone else has to catch the ball, make the throw, or get a hit. Lefty understood the idea of teamwork.

On the mountain it was vitally important to remember that we were climbing as a group, not simply as a group of individuals. Who we were as a whole superseded who we were as individuals. While it was true that each of us had to carry his or her load, and we all had to take our own steps, nonetheless, we traveled as a team of climbers. This "we" included everyone—climbers, guides, and porters—because our success rested with each other.

I have always liked the proverb that says, "Don't buy the house; buy the neighborhood." It reminds me that we live in community. *E Pluribus Unum.*

EPILOGUE

Traveling is glamorous only in retrospect.
—Paul Theroux

As I look back on my journey to the summit of Kilimanjaro, I see a set of life lessons that can be applied to help meet any of life's mountains. When faced with an opportunity or challenge . . .

• **Set a goal.** Whatever the situation might be—getting a job, earning a degree, healing a troubled marriage, beating cancer, or dealing with the grief of loss—a person can use that moment as an opportunity to set a clear goal. "In the long run, men hit only what they aim at," observed Henry David Thoreau. Goals give direction and purpose to life. In the final analysis, reaching a goal is not nearly as important as having one for which to reach. In the story of Alice in Wonderland, there is a moment where Alice comes to a crossroads and does not know which way to go. The Cheshire Cat asks her, "Where are you going?"

"I'm not quite sure," she says in reply.

"Then," counsels the cat, "any road will do."

Having a clear goal or set of goals in mind does not give the traveler a detailed map for the journey, but it does determine the direction he or she moves and also provides a compass for navigation.

• **Go with a guide.** I suppose a person could argue that having arrived at the base of Kilimanjaro, from where the peak could be clearly seen, would eliminate the need for a guide. All a climber would need to do would be to simply walk from that spot to the top. I found out on many occasions, however, just how important it is to have a guide. Seeing the mountain and knowing it are two different things. The twists and turns, the places to find water and shade, the best way to make the final ascent, are all things learned over time. On several occasions my whole confidence rested in putting my foot where the foot of my guide had been.

• **Go with a group.** Having others with you as you navigate the ups and downs of life has a way of multiplying your joy and dividing grief. John Donne was right, "No man [or woman] is an island." We are individuals, but we live in community for a reason. Others help us see ourselves and be ourselves. The mutual accountability of a family or a congregation or a team of coworkers helps bring out the best in each individual.

• **Prepare for the journey.** There are times when we know that a particular challenge awaits us. In those moments, we have the opportunity to assemble the resources and knowledge needed to meet the test. On other occasions, however, the mountain appears with little or no notice. A phone call, a doctor's visit, or a sudden accident can put us face-to-face with a seemingly overwhelming challenge. Because life is unpredictable, we must, as much as possible, live ready. The Boy Scouts have a simple motto, which can be applied to life itself. It is this: "Be Prepared." It wasn't raining when Noah built the ark.

• **Keep looking up.** "The future is purchased by the present," observed Samuel Johnson. As you climb a great mountain, there are vistas at nearly every turn. It is right and good to pause along the way to look back to see from where you have come, to look to the right and left to see the unfolding landscape all around; but the set of your gaze must remain always upward. A person dare not live his or her life looking only in the rearview mirror or staring out the window. Having a goal will mean little to a person if that goal ceases to be the object of his or her vision.

- **Travel lightly.** There is no reason and little wisdom in carrying more than what is needed for the journey. Americans, bred by a consumer culture, often live cluttered lives. When that happens, our possessions end up possessing us. Traveling light includes casting off your disappointments, laying aside your frustrations, and putting your faith in God for strength and comfort. The mountains of life become more manageable when the load a person carries is lightened.

- **Maintain your balance.** The edge of a mountain is no place for someone with two left feet. The margin for error is too small. Balance is important not only physically but also emotionally and mentally as a person seeks to overcome a challenge or difficulty. There will be highs and lows, and the ability to maintain an inner calm and a clear faith in God is critical. The same balance I needed on the climb is needed in my daily life as well.

- **Stay flexible.** Things change. Even the best-laid plans of mice and men have a way of getting interrupted. There are moments when everything goes well in life, but those moments don't last long. Change is imbedded in the nature of being alive. Therefore, being flexible and willing to adjust to the twists and turns of life enables a person to continue to make progress even in the face of added challenges or obstacles. Hannibal, the great conqueror, said, "We will either find a way, or make one." And he did; and so can we, if we stay focused and flexible.

- **Don't put yourself in danger.** This may seem like an odd principle for one who climbed a mountain. Climbing Kilimanjaro was itself a dangerous act; but even so, there were things I could do to minimize the danger. I remember several times along the climb when I had to resist the temptation to jump across a crevasse rather than to slowly work my way down around and back up. I recall a particular moment on the Barranco Wall when I realized that one misstep would mean serious injury; so I altered my pace and used both hands to grip the rock.

Life by its very nature is dangerous. Cars wreck; people get sick; earthquakes and hurricanes happen. We cannot live danger-free; but there are times when we have choices and in those moments we need to keep ourselves from danger—fasten our seat belts, wash our hands, turn away from temptation.

• **Get up every time you fall down!** Being a student, a former college faculty member, and now a university president, I have sat through scores of graduation ceremonies and listened to countless commencement speeches, some of them my own. I have observed certain principles that seem universally true.

First, no one comes just to hear the speech. The students are there to receive their diplomas; their friends and families are there to celebrate the moment; and faculty members attend to observe the fruit of their labor. Generally, it is only the speaker who has come solely for the speech.

Second, it is my judgment that shorter is generally better. The shortest commencement speech I know of was delivered by Sir Winston Churchill, the valiant prime minister of Great Britain during World War II. After a lengthy introduction and a thunderous round of applause, the diminutive statesman walked to the podium, gazed for a long moment into the faces of the graduates, and said, "Never give up. Never give up. Never give up." With that, he turned and walked back to his seat.

I was the first of our group to fall. However, being the first to fall also meant I was the first to pick myself up and keep going. It's not the fall that matters; it's the getting up that counts!

A FINAL WORD

*He who forms the mountains, creates the wind, and reveals his thoughts to man, he who turns dawn into darkness, and treads the high places of the earth—the L*ORD *God Almighty is his name.*
—Amos 4:13

NOTES

1. Isak Dinesen, *Out of Africa* (1952; reprint, New York: Random House, 2002), 68.

2. Audrey Salkeld, *Kilimanjaro: To the Roof of Africa* (Washington, D.C.: National Geographic Books, 2001), 45.

3. Quoted in Cameron M. Burns, *Kilimanjaro and Mount Kenya: A Climbing and Trekking Guide* (Seattle: The Mountaineers, 1998), 14.

4. Hans Meyer, *Across East African Glaciers*, quoted in Henry Stedman, *Kilimanjaro—A Trekking Guide to Africa's Highest Mountain* (Surrey, U.K.: Trailblazer Publications, 2003), 38.

5. Neville Shulman in the foreword to Stephen Carmichael and Susan Stoddard, *Climbing Mount Kilimanjaro* (Bloomington, Ill.: Medi-Ed Press, 2002), 11.

6. Nikolaus Lenau, quoted in David Kundtz, *Everyday Serenity: Meditations for People Who Do Too Much* (New York: MJF Books, 2000), 226.

7. James Stanley Gilbert, "To the Southern Cross," in *Panama Patchwork: Poems* (n.p., 1909), 17.

8. Lorne A. Adrain, *The Most Important Thing I Know About . . .* (Kansas City: Andrews McMeel Publishing, 2001), 59.

9. Peter Friederici, "Fifteen Ways of Seeing Light," in *The Best Spiritual Writing 2004*, Philip Zaleski, ed. (New York: Houghton Mifflin, 2004), 82.

10. Stephen Vincent Benet, quoted in Kundtz, *Everyday Serenity*, 186.

11. Sidney Lovett, quoted in *Graduation Moments* (Tulsa: Bordon Books, 2004), 82.

12. Kundtz, *Everyday Serenity*, 242.

13. From the poem "High Flight," which was a part of a letter written by John Gillespie Magee Jr. to his parents during World War II. The letter is dated September 3, 1941. Magee was a young airman in the war. He died a few months later on December 11, 1941. He was an American, born in China of missionary parents. This quotation was made famous by President Ronald Reagan who used a portion of it in his speech to the nation following the explosion of the U.S. Space Shuttle *Challenger* in January of 1986. The poem can be found at <www.highflightproductions.com>.

14. Ibid., 7.

15. Mother Teresa, quoted in ibid., 184.

16. Marian Edelman, quoted in ibid., 342.

17. Tim O'Brien, *The Things They Carried* (New York: Broadway Books, 1990), 1-2.

18. Brennan Manning, *Lion and Lamb: The Relentless Tenderness of Jesus* (Grand Rapids: Chosen Books, 1986), 129-30.

19. Raymon Inmon, *The Most Brilliant Thoughts of All Time,* John M. Shanahan, ed. (New York City: Cliff Street Books, 1999), 289.

20. William Wordsworth, *The Prelude* in *The Complete Poetical Works of William Wordsworth,* introduced by John Morley (London: MacMillan, 1950), 261.

21. Kundtz, *Everyday Serenity,* 364-65.